The Service Business Money Machine

How to Easily Turn Your Website into a

Job-Getting, Deal-Closing, 24/7 Money-Making Machine

By: Joe Burnich

"How do you eat an elephant?
One bite at a time! That's how you
should approach your marketing."

– Unknown

The Service Business Money Machine

How to Easily Turn Your Website into a Job-Getting, Deal-Closing, 24/7 Money-Making Machine

By: Joe Burnich

Published in the United States of America by

Big West Marketing, Inc.
913 SW Higgins Ave
Missoula, MT 59803

ISBN-13:978-1544845326
ISBN-10:1544845324

To contact the office Joe Burnich for a free consultation, please call:

406-493-1881
or visit
www.BigWestMarketing.com

Dedicated to my amazing daughters, Camila and Sofia.

Contents

Introduction to Your Success Story

The purpose of this book is simple: I want to show you how to set up your website so that it will be the most valuable part of your business. I want to show you how to take it from being an online brochure to being a money-making machine that works for you 24/7 to generate new customers, phone calls and jobs. I want your website to set you free from the tedious work of Internet marketing so you can focus on running and growing your business the way you want to.

I want to help you succeed!

You may think you've tried it all or heard it all when it comes to Internet marketing. I'm about to share how you can set up hands-off marketing and reveal little-known tips to get lots of calls for your business. First, however, I'm going to share a rather embarrassing story with you.

I wasn't always a web design and SEO expert. And I certainly wasn't a guy to be featured in trade magazines, podcasts and invited to speak at entrepreneur groups like the national *1 Million Cups.* My business story has some humble beginnings. I remember it was April 2009 and frankly, one of the lowest points of my life. As is often the case, it was hitting rock bottom that led me to where I am today.

My wife, 10-month-old baby daughter and I decided to move from Kansas City back to Missoula, Montana where I grew up as a child. We wanted a safe place to raise kids and help out with my 80-year-old grandmother who was still living in Missoula. So we loaded up our beat-up minivan and made the move with only few thousand dollars in savings.

Here is a picture of my family in the early days 2009:

I had no job and no prospects.

My background is in customer service and graphic design. I soon learned the job market in Montana was absolutely horrible. I couldn't find a decent job to save my life.

This terrifying question kept coming up: How am I going to support my new family?

(406) 493-1881

Luckily, I connected with Rick Kern, a longtime family friend who suggested I start a cleaning service business to make some extra money. We both thought it would be temporary until I could find a good job and get on my feet. So I pulled my meager savings out of the bank, bought some used equipment and loaded up the minivan.

I was excited to be in business for myself and ready for the work to start rolling in.

That didn't happen. In fact, the bills were piling up, the debt was increasing and the phone was not ringing. I resorted to working part-time for my landlord cutting grass and painting apartments just to make sure the rent was paid. I was struggling. Anybody who has been a similar situation knows how embarrassing it is when you can't support your own family.

Then it got worse…

I remember that it was cold, wet and a little gloomy. My wife, baby and I were driving our little beat-up minivan home from Pizza Hut where we had used a coupon for a rare night out. We were about two blocks away from our apartment when I felt a sharp pain in my gut. At first I thought it was nothing, but it continued throughout the night and was getting worse.

Finally, at three o'clock in the morning the pain was unbearable. I didn't want to wake the baby so I jumped in the minivan and drove myself to the emergency room.

After spending twelve hours in agonizing pain and having doctors and nurses stick me with needles and shove various tubes in and out of my body, they diagnosed me with Crohn's Disease (later it turned out to be Celiac Disease). And on top of that, I found out my temporary health insurance was going to expire the next month and there was no money to renew the plan.

So let's recap: I had a struggling business that was barely paying the bills, I was diagnosed with a nasty disease and I couldn't afford to support my family. I felt hopeless and trapped. How was I going to get myself out of this situation as broke as I was?

The thing about utter desperation is that sometimes it focuses the mind. Lying in that hospital bed waiting to be discharged, something happened in my head and my heart. I decided at that very moment: "I will NEVER EVER feel this way again. I will figure this out and take my family out of this situation…no matter what!" It wasn't a matter of "If", it was a matter of "How".

It was only a few days later that I was again talking with my friend, Rick Kern. We were discussing how to make my struggling business really take off. We knew we needed to get the word out, but advertising was too expensive. I had already built my own website using my graphic design skills, but nobody was visiting the website so it wasn't doing me much good.

At the time, Rick was making some good money with an online business selling pre-paid cell phones. He introduced me to the concept of Search Engine Optimization (SEO), which basically is what allows your website to rank high on Google when someone types in a specific search term. We decided that improving the ranking for my local business on Google might bring in some more work.

Rick taught me the basics of SEO and I ran with it.

The thing about SEO is that it typically takes several months to see results. Every morning before anybody else was up, I would jump on the computer and do everything possible to learn and implement SEO. Then during the day, I would be out pounding the pavement, going door-to-door trying to drum up work. I also borrowed some money to pay for a local coupon mail-out.

And guess what? Work finally started coming in.

Four months after I started working on SEO, my website hit the bottom of the first page of the Google search results and I started to get a few calls. The next month I was in the middle of the page and calls increased. After six months, my website was bouncing around the top three positions. The calls were really coming in now.

I had made it. I was back on top. I was paying my bills and supporting my family. I no longer felt trapped and I felt true freedom: the freedom of running my own successful business.

As the years went on, I continued to run my business and on the side, I helped other service businesses with their websites and SEO. What I began to realize was that a lot of business owners didn't really like the marketing side of business. They just wanted to work and run their business. I, on the other hand, liked marketing more than any other aspect.

As my marketing side-hustle expanded, I realized I would have to focus if I really wanted to grow. I sold my cleaning business to a friend in 2014 so all my energy would go to my new company, Big West Marketing.

At the time of writing this book, we have an office and dedicated team of five amazing people. We have helped over 850 service businesses with their websites, marketing and SEO needs.

Remember, despite my success today, I'm really no different than anyone else. I'm just a guy who stumbled upon a really effective system and worked hard to make it work. And it's the same exact system I'll be sharing with you in this book, so you can finally experience freedom and results like these for yourself!

Is This Book for You?

Answer these questions:
- Are you a business owner looking for more customers online?
- Do you currently have a website but not enough traffic or people contacting you to use your services?
- Are you overwhelmed and confused by all the options online for marketing your business?
- Are you too busy running your business to focus time and energy on website marketing?
- Are you bombarded with dozens of phone calls from salespeople trying to sell you marketing schemes, done-for-you web templates, SEO or other online marketing programs?
- Do you know that more and more people are going online to find services you offer but you haven't been able capture a piece of this massive opportunity?
- Are you looking for a solution to simplify and automate all this online marketing stuff?

If any or all of these questions are answered with a "YES" and you want to stand out in your local area as the top service provider, then this book is for you!

This book will provide a simple step-by-step proven blueprint to help you quickly and easily turn your website into a virtual money-making machine.

Who Should Not Read This Book?

Most small business owners I have met are some of the best, down-to-earth, hardest-working individuals on the planet, but there are some shady characters out there.
- If you are looking to make a quick buck, then this book is not for you.

- If you make money off of "bait-and-switch" tactics, then this book is not for you.
- If you aren't willing to do the work to build a foundation of satisfied customers, then this book is not for you.

This book is for any business owner that wants to build a proud, reputable business in their community. This book is for any business owner that cares about the quality of service they provide. This book is for any business owner that cares about the customer and has do-whatever-it-takes attitude (even during the slow season) to get business.

If that sounds like you, then you are going to love what I have to say.

Why Did I Write This Book?

In my many years of helping hundreds of service and contract businesses get more calls, leads, jobs, customers and money through smart web design and search engine ranking, I realized three common truths:

1. Service business owners (like you) are highly-skilled technicians. They are amazing at what they do and take pride in a job well done.
2. The laser focus on the technical side of the business leaves little time for a marketing. They are so busy working *IN* the business they don't have time to work *ON* the business. They end up settling for websites that looks nice, but do not get traffic and convert visitors into paying customers.
3. Virtually every business owner I speak to is overwhelmed with all the tedious Internet stuff. It is called "Too Much Information." They just don't have the time, desire or mental energy to both run a successful business and worry about all

the 1000s of ideas when it comes to websites and Internet marketing programs.

Based on these truths, it is my goal to demystify website confusion. I want to cut through the noise and BS and give you "The Meat" - you know, the stuff that actually works. I didn't fill this book with lots of clever ideas and information that sounds good but has never been tested. I'm going to give you the stuff I know works for sure. I use it on my websites and my client's websites. This is real-world stuff that you can implement today!

I was first inspired to write this book by my friend and mentor, Mark Kennedy, who was one of the first in the industry to write a comprehensive book on running a successful service business. I learned so much from his book back in 2010, but I never thought I would be motivated to write a book of my own.

Five years later another industry friend, Deon Bush, published his own book and encouraged me to do the same. It took a while for me to test and implement the techniques and tips I wanted to share. Now here I am with my own book, hoping that you get massive value from these pages just as I did from the books I've read throughout the years.

Beware, I'm not a professional writer and I don't play one on the Internet. If you're looking for good grammar or perfect literary structure, then please close this book right now. I'm a normal guy who, after being confused, frustrated and burned by "Internet Marketers," I decided to take matters into my own hands and test, test and do more testing until I got it right.

My message is one of hope. I have been where you are now, and I had mentors and guides who helped me shorten the learning curve. If you have been searching for a solution to building your service business and are willing to put in some time and effort, then please accept my help. You will be glad you did.

Does that mean my knowledge is 100% complete? No, I don't know it all, but I'm damn sure I know more than anyone else in the industry when it comes to smart web design, SEO and what really works. That said, if someone can prove me wrong or come up with a better proven solution (that is backed up with actual data), then I will be the first admit it. Like I said, this book is all about the stuff that works!

What Makes This Book Different?

There is endless information on the subject of website design, Internet marketing, SEO, Google rankings, etc. But one thing I see missing is specific information for specific industries. These "experts" give broad general marketing advice that assumes every business should market the same way. Many times, they don't distinguish the difference between marketing a small local business and marketing a BIG multi-national corporation. They bunch everything together as if it's all the same thing.

I'm here to tell you first hand that marketing a national company and a local business are two completely different animals. And to take it a step further, effective marketing strategies for different types of local businesses can be very different as well. Do you think a marketing strategy for a local coffee shop, jewelry store and carpet cleaner should be implemented the same way? Absolutely not!

Admittedly there is some overlap and general marketing principles that can be applied to a variety of different business types. However, the actionable day-to-day strategies will vary greatly. My company only works with businesses in the service or contractor industry. This puts me in unique position to help you.

This book is specifically for service based businesses. Your business goes into people's homes and businesses to provide a service. It is important that you create a connection with the people you serve. They must know, like and trust that you are who you say you are and that you will do what you say you will do. The marketing of small service companies is similar because we want to create a relationship based on trust and quality.

Everything you will learn in this book is based on building that trust and showing potential customers that you are a quality company.

What You Are Going To Get Out Of This Book

I'm going to cover a specific blueprint and checklist for getting two, three or even ten times more business from your website. We've completed hundreds of websites for service businesses over the years. Our company has been testing different variables to see what really works…what really gets the phone to ring.

Most business owners and marketers (and web designers) have no idea what really works when it comes to conversion (an industry term for converting advertising and marketing into active clients). They have opinions and ideas, but no real data to back it up. They focus on things that have little to no impact on actual customer acquisition. And let's be honest, no matter how attractive or how many bells and whistles your website has, if it's not bringing in the most calls possible, then what's the point?

And I'm as guilty as any small business owner and/or web designer reading this book. I didn't know what I didn't know. When I first started my service business, my goal was to have the coolest website in town. I just wanted to impress people.

Now, I have to say the web sites we build are pretty damn cool in my opinion, but over the years I've switched my focus to function over form.

I want sites that perform. So should you. Period.

Think about this: If you take all the testing, data and analysis from 100s of sever business websites, it would take years to figure out the stuff I'm about to share. I want to cut down on your learning curve.

Obviously, you are a smart and ambitious business owner, or you would not be reading this book. I want to congratulate you and encourage you to incorporate these steps and systems towards a more successful business.

Bottom line is that there is a specific formula to hit certain psychological triggers that get people to take action. This is really simple stuff, but most people don't know about it, or are unwilling to take the time to put it into practice - just like I didn't know a few years ago.

Depending on your situation, you can do this yourself or have your web designer do this for you. You should be able to make changes quick and easy. If you need help understanding or implementing anything in this book you can visit our website, YouTube channel, Facebook page, or just email or call our office for a free consultation.

At first this might seem like a lot of information. You don't have to implement everything right away, but the more you do, the better your results will be. Every step will move you closer to success.

Let's get a quick overview.

This Book is Divided into Three Sections:

1. **<u>Website Usability:</u>** Is your website clear and usable? Is it obvious what you are about and what the visitor should do? Can they easily find what they are looking for without scrolling and searching? I will show you how to make your website functional, user-friendly and action-oriented.

2. **<u>Website Trust:</u>** Are you establishing trust with your visitors? Do they see you as a friendly face? Are you recognized as the best provider in your community? I will show you how to gain visitors' trust and turn them into paying customers.

3. **<u>Website Traffic:</u>** Websites need traffic. How many eyeballs are on your website every month? How are people finding your website? I have found that ranking on Google and marketing on Facebook are the best ways to get traffic to your website. I will show you how to capitalize on both.

So, when we put usability, trust and traffic all together, it results in an explosion of phone calls and new customers. We will cover all this and more to make your website the best it can possibly be. You are now on your way to building your own *Service Business Money Machine.*

Let's get started!

Chapter 1:

The Power of Making It Easy

If someone lands on your website, you have to engage them in a way that addresses their problem and speaks to their needs in a clear way. You only have a few seconds to get their attention before they decide to move on to a competitor's site. You may know what a great job you do and how your method is superior, but this is not about ego, it is about engagement.

Let Them Know What You Do

The first thing you need to do is tell them what you do. You have to let them know they came to the right place. If your site is unclear, too cluttered, or complicated, they will NOT have that feeling. They will have a bad user experience. It is very important to understand that even a professional-looking website does not solve this problem.

With all the do-it-yourself, ready-to-go website templates that exist on the market these days, it's easy to assume that your slick new website is ready to go. If it looks good to you and your friends, you may expect the phone to start ringing with new business. Most of the time this is not the case.

(406) 493-1881

To the customer looking for a local company, you are a just another local business that joined the crowded Internet space. You may know you and your service are unique, your references outstanding and your price fair. But most of the time that is not effectively communicated on the website. The key is to set you, the business owner, apart with a simple yet strategic plan. So, where do we start?

In our testing of hundreds of service-based websites, we have determined that simple is best. To start, you need a Logo and/or Business Name that clearly states what you do. If you tell a complete stranger your business name, is it obvious to them what you do? If you show a complete stranger your logo, is it obvious to them what you do? Is your name, logo and business one that comes instantly to mind when someone asks for a referral?

Never assume anything. Ask ten strangers: "what do you think of when you hear my business name?" Ask ten strangers: "what they think of when they see your logo?"

If you are just starting out and don't have a business name yet then think about this before making a final decision. Come up with a few names and ask your friends and family if each one makes sense.

Now, I am not saying that you need to change your business name if you are an established business. Instead, if your logo or business name does not clearly explain what you do, then you can simply implement a clear, concise tagline or slogan to add to the website (and to your business cards). Something like:

"Top-Rated Carpet Cleaner in Kansas City"

—or —

"Best HVAC Service in Los Angeles"

Don't make them guess what you are all about. If you provide lots of different services, just pick the most important for this section. Make your offer simple and obvious; don't try to be too clever at this point. If you want to be clever, wait until we get to chapter 6, which deals with Trust Elements.

Make It Easy To Contact You

Now that the mystery is gone and they know what you do and know they are in the right place, make it easy for them to contact you.

It's important to understand that very few people have the time or the desire to read through all the pages of your website. This is especially true when it comes to people viewing your website on their smart phones. In fact, most people don't even scroll down the Home page. So, it is crucial that you get them to take action right away.

How do we do this?

(406) 493-1881

You need a **Big Bold** phone number at the top of EVERY page. Don't make them search. This means no tiny phone numbers, or phone numbers only on the Contact page. If they don't see your phone number within three seconds, then you are doing it wrong. The phone number should be THE most important part of any service website.

Here is a good rule of thumb: If you stand 10 feet from your computer and look at your website, does the phone number pop out? Check it out right now! Pull your website up, step back and check it out. Does it pass the test? If the answer is "No", then make it bigger and make the color of the phone number stand out from the rest of the site.

Let people know that you are easy to connect with and contact. Remember, we want a good user experience. We don't want them to feel frustrated before they even call you.

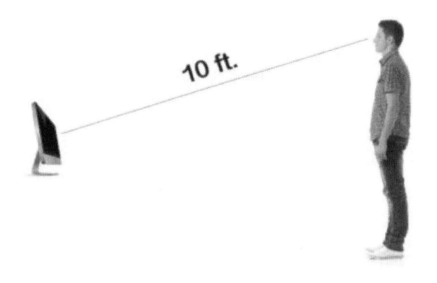

Furthermore, a large percentage of visitors don't want to read text, research your company, look at pictures, watch videos etc. They want a phone number of someone who can solve their problem. They want to talk to a person who comes across as trustworthy and easy to work with.

This one simple tweak can double or triple your website response rate. Its sounds too easy, but believe me, this is powerful stuff that most people don't think about.

Now let's put turbo boosters on that phone number with a clear call-to-action.

Clear Call-To-Action

Along with the phone number, there should always be a Call-To-Action. Don't over-think this one. Keep it short and sweet. Simply tell them what to do.

(406) 493-1881

Examples: *"Call Now!"* or my favorite: *"Free Estimate. Call Now!"*

Most business owners think, "Well, if my phone number is on the site, they know what to do. I don't need to tell them what to do." Don't be so sure. My experience and the data from numerous marketing studies show that this one little tweak can double or triple calls. Watch those late night infomercials; they always have a call-to-action. The reason they sell millions of dollars in junk that nobody needs is because they are always telling people what to do. And they make it very simple to connect **right now.**

This goes for all marketing, not only your website. You will want to add it to your business cards, van wraps, postcards, billboards, etc. Frequent and basic calls-to-action are psychological triggers – very simple stuff that makes your phone number much more powerful. It really is like putting turbo boosters on your website.

Contact Forms

In addition to big bold phone numbers and calls-to-action, it's also helpful to have simple contact forms on every page of your website. Your clients, existing and new, will have different communication styles, so make it easy for them to contact you in many various ways.

A contact form is just a website form that allows people to enter their contact information and then send it to your email inbox. This has nothing to do with complicated price calculators or automatic responding programs. You are simply giving an alternative to calling your phone number.

Many websites have a contact form on their Contact Us page only. But once again, that is making it difficult for people to get hold of you. Don't make them search or click around to find this form. Think about how many times you have become frustrated with trying to connect with someone and have chosen another provider.

(406) 493-1881

Why would someone use the form instead of just picking up the phone? Most people will contact you by phone if you follow my previous advice. However, some people are analytical and are in research mode and aren't ready to pick up the phone quite yet. They feel more comfortable reaching out with the form. Or it may be late at night when they find your site or perhaps they work at an office where personal phone calls are not allowed.

In our experience, 1 out 10 people use the form as opposed to the phone number. If I didn't have a contact form on my site, then our business would be potentially losing 10% of visitors looking for the services that we offer. That can add up to a serious loss of profit over time.

What should this form look like? Keep it short, with no more than 4 or 5 fields. I like to ask for the name, phone, email, best time to call and what service they are interested in. Anything more than that will reduce the number of people who use it.

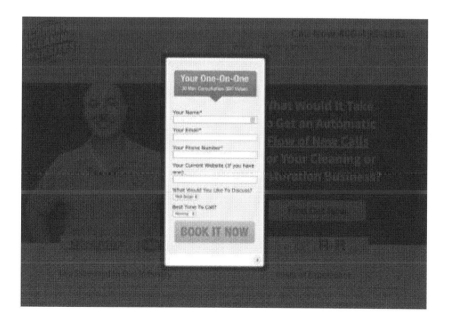

The primary objective is to get some basic information and start a conversation. I recommend against using email to give bids or estimates.

Once you have their phone number, call them or use the email exchange to set up a call appointment. When you have a conversation, you are establishing a live connection. It is too easy to ignore an email. You want to build repeat customers who will refer you to other repeat customers, and you do this by establishing a relationship.

In summary, you have just a few seconds to convey what you do and how they can contact you for more information. If you have these crucial areas covered, then you will be way ahead of 90% of all service websites on the Internet.

These are simple changes that you or your web designer can make within a few minutes. In the next chapter, we will discuss how to make it easy for the visitor to find exactly what they want quickly and easily. You are going to discover *"How to Easily Turn Your Website Into a Job-Getting, Deal- Closing, 24/7 Money-Making Machine"* by correctly setting up the menus and pages.

Chapter 1 Action Steps:

Make sure your business name and logo clearly explain what you do. If they don't, create a simple descriptive slogan or tagline.

Make sure your phone number is BIG and BOLD and appears at the top of EVERY page of your website.

Make sure you have a contact form on EVERY page of your website.

NOTES:

Chapter 2:

Navigation Menus and Pages

You want to give your visitors a seamless experience which makes it easy for them to get around your website. In order to do this, you need to correctly set up your navigation menus and pages. In this chapter, you are going to learn methods that are the most effective ways to accomplish this.

Navigation Menus

A navigation menu is a list or group of links that direct visitors to different pages and sections without scrolling. You want the viewer to find exactly what they want as quickly and painlessly as possible. Some sites may use a single primary navigation bar on each page. Some choose to use a primary navigation bar on the home page and then secondary bars on others.

In my experience, I find that the most effective navigation menus are horizontal and are placed at the very top of the website or directly below the header image. And most importantly, they need to be on every page, not just the Home page.

Ever since the first websites started showing up on the Internet, people have been trained to look for horizontal menu bars to navigate around a website and find the pages they want. Some web designers try to do all kinds of variations with vertical menus, toggle menus, slide-in or pop-out menus. Although some of those fancy menus look really cool, testing has shown that effectiveness decreases.

Remember, we want stuff that works. Avoid that which is complicated or confusing.

Don't make the visitor work to find what they want. Additional navigation with graphics or animations are fine, but only as a supplement for the horizontal menu, not a substitution. After the navigation menu is set up, then it is time to decide on which pages we will add to the menu to make your website succeed.

The Three Essential Pages

To begin, let's consider three main questions most visitors will have when landing on a local service website: Who are you? What do you do? Can I trust you?
It's easy to get carried away when deciding which pages to include on your website.

In addition to the Home page these important questions should be answered with three essential pages:

1. About Us Page (who are you?)
2. Services Page (what do you do?)
3. Testimonials Page (can I trust you?)

The About Us Page

Many business owners take the "About Us" page for granted and it ends up just telling what you do rather than who you are. That is unfortunate because analytics reveal the "About Us" page as one of the most visited pages on any website. In addition to your "Testimonials" page, this is an important opportunity to make a connection and build trust.

My advice is to focus on the things that make you human. Tell your story by answering these questions:
1. How did you get started in the business?

2.   What makes your company different from your competitors?

3.   What is your opinion on customer service and how do you treat your current clients?

The idea is to let them know who you are as a person and as a company. Make it warm and conversational as if you were sitting at a table with a client telling them about yourself and what you are all about.

It is also very powerful to include one or more personal pictures of you, your crew, your family, your pets, etc. We will get more into personalization in the section on trust, but this is a great place to start.

The Services Page

The "Services" page should be set up in one of two ways, depending on how many services you offer. If you offer one service with several variations, then you can have one dedicated page explaining everything in detail. If you have multiple services, each one needs its own page. This is important for both clarity and Search Engine Optimization (SEO). Each of the service pages should be displayed as a dropdown menu under the main navigation menu.

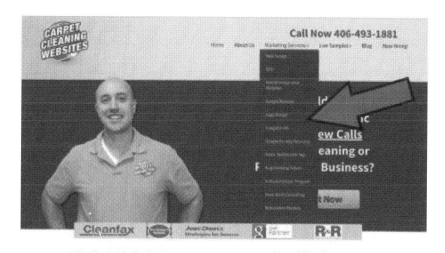

The Testimonials Page

Also known as the "Customer Reviews" page, the "Testimonials" page is where visitors go to see rave reviews from past customers. It builds credibility and trust. Simple text-based testimonials are fine and are definitely better than nothing, but the most effective testimonials will be joined by a photo of the reviewer. I call these "Power Reviews". And if you really want to take it up a level use video testimonials. Some people may be reluctant to share their full name, but most will share their first name and the city where they live.

"Just what I was looking for. This company is really wonderful and they provide top-notch service. The technicians arrived on time and were very attentive to our needs. They went above and beyond during the entire process. Highly recommended. Thank you for making it painless, pleasant and most of all hassle-free!"
- Julie Y.

The "Home," "About Us," "Services" and "Testimonials" pages will make for a complete website. Additional pages can be effective depending on your marketing strategy. Let's look at some of these pages in detail.

The Optional Special Offers Page

Another important page I would like to discuss is the Special Offers page. This is a controversial topic as most marketing experts warn against putting discounts, coupons or specials on advertising. Their argument is that it cheapens your service, causes price wars and encourages price shopping, and that is true to a certain extent. However, the decision to include a Specials Page depends on your business model and your personality type.

I know some business owners that refuse to put any kind of pricing anywhere on their website or advertising and they do very well. Others will put special offers all over the website including the "Home" page and are also very successful. So which model should you choose?

In our business, we have tried both models with great success and it all came down to one question: How busy are we right now and can we handle more customers with the same amount of care and consideration that is our standard? Remember, the great part about advertising with a website is that you can change things on the fly anytime you want to. Unlike a static ad in a phone book or directory, you have the flexibility to easily test, assess and regroup.

What Is a Blog Page And Do I Need One?

A blog is simply a website page that is continually updated with new articles or posts. There is a lot of misinformation in the world of Internet marketing about blogs. Some people claim that you must have a blog that is constantly updated in order to rank on Google. I can tell you first hand that this is a myth, especially when it comes to a local business website.

At one point we conducted a test on over 30 different client sites by adding a unique blog post every week for over six months to see what effect it would have on Google rankings. The results showed that it had no effect. So why would someone choose to have a blog?

The purpose of a blog is to provide new and useful information to your clients, much like an online newspaper or magazine. I personally use a blog on my website because I am constantly informing my clients and prospects of new updates or changes in the world of web design and Internet marketing.

Does this mean you should do the same? Only if you enjoy writing articles and have a steady stream of fresh information to share with people. The typical local service business will not have the time or desire to constantly write new articles.

(406) 493-1881

So, is it essential to the success of your website? **Absolutely not.** Can it be helpful if you enjoy writing articles on a continual basis? Possibly, but don't depend on it, as it won't affect SEO.

Other Pages

Most other pages are considered bonus information. They are not essential to the website, but can be helpful as support pages. Here are some examples of other pages you could have on your website:

- Contact Us
- Service Area
- FAQ
- Tips
- Photo Gallery
- Video Gallery
- Our Process
- Now Hiring

These bonus pages also come in handy to decrease the amount of time you spend talking with potential clients on the phone. If the potential client is one of the few people that really want to research your services, methods, processes, etc., they can read about it before they call you.

You can also direct people to certain pages instead of spending valuable time answering questions, explaining and re-explaining.

Once your website has been properly set up with menus and pages, it's time to consider how the site will appear on smartphones and mobile devices. In the next chapter, we will discuss how to make sure your website is set up for mobile success. This is just one more step in developing your *Money Machine*.

Chapter 2 Action Steps:

Make sure you have a horizontal navigation menu at the top of EVERY page.

In addition to the Home page make sure you include the three essential pages:

- About Us
- Services
- Testimonials

Decide if you want to have a Special offers page and any other educational pages that might help the customer pick up the phone and call.

NOTES:

Chapter 3:

Going Mobile

At the time of this writing, Google reports that over 60% of consumers are searching for local service businesses on their smart phones. Our experience shows the percentage is much higher in some cities. Mediative.com reports that 89% of participants admitted to searching for a local business on their smartphone once a week or more, with 58% searching at least daily.

This information alone can put your business a cut above the competition. This means your site must be either be mobile responsive or must redirect to a separate mobile site if it's pulled up on a smartphone or tablet. If you don't make these changes, conversions will most likely drop, and so will your rankings. Google now actually penalizes sites that are not mobile friendly. We've seen sites drop 10 spots or more. This is very important for usability and for getting ranked on Google.

How To Know If Your Website Is Mobile Ready

Many people think that just because their website shrinks down and shows up a smartphone that their website is mobile ready. This is not always the case. As with other business principles, it is very important to never assume anything. Even if your web designer says your website is mobile friendly, you should still verify for yourself. Many web designers are technically inclined, but are not trained in online marketing and the best practices for reaching your customers.

All you need to do is go to Google and search for "Mobile Website Testing Tool." This is a free tool that Google provides and it only takes a couple minutes. You can even show your webmaster and teach him or her a thing or two.

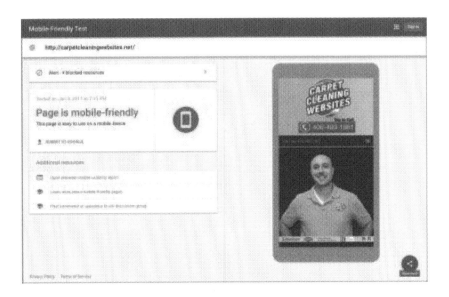

Mobile Website Vs. Mobile Responsive Website

When it comes to mobile websites there are two options, each with their own advantages and disadvantages. Both options will pass the Google mobile test, so from an SEO standpoint they are both viable. The one you choose will depend on your specific needs.

1. **The Separate Mobile Website**
    The first option is to create a separate mobile website. This means when someone lands on your website, they will be automatically redirected to a completely different website that

(406) 493-1881

is created specifically for a mobile device. It will have its own unique website address that most of the time is a sub-domain of your primary domain. It will look something like this: m.yourwebsite.com.

If you don't understand this technical jargon, don't worry, it's not essential information. I just wanted to throw it in for those that want a detailed explanation. Any qualified web designer will understand exactly what I'm talking about.

Years ago when smartphones first started becoming popular, the separate mobile website was the only option. Big West Marketing has created hundreds of these mobile sites, but in my opinion it is the "old way." It can work for your business, as it did for us in the beginning, but we have since moved to the responsive option for all new clients. I will explain both options in detail so you can make the best choice.

The primary advantage to choosing a separate mobile website is that you have complete control in customizing the site to look and function exactly as you want. The big disadvantage is that you will have to maintain two separate websites. So whenever you make an update or change to your desktop website, you will have to remember to make the changes on the mobile website as well.

This can be problematic since you (or your web designer) will be working on two separate platforms. It will increase the amount of time and/or money spent on updating or maintaining your website.

2.   The Mobile Responsive Website
These days a fully responsive website is the most popular way to go. Instead of redirecting the visitor to a separate mobile

website, your current website will simply respond to the screen size and reorder itself to appear favorably on any device.

Although you won't have as much control over how the mobile version looks or functions, you will still have the advantage of maintaining a single website. For a service business, this should be more than sufficient. There are only very special cases where a business would want complete control over the mobile site. An example would be if you sell physical products online.

Since we are talking about a service-based business, it is my advice to make life easy and go with the mobile responsive option.

Regardless of which option you choose, your primary goal is to get people to call. Many business owners astound me by forgetting that phone calls are the way the money flows in. Web designers completely ignore this fact and are looking at the technical side of the website as opposed to the marketing potential.

On many mobile sites or responsive sites, you will find that the phone number is not even clickable; it's tiny or just represented by a little icon. Rarely is it at the very top of the site and rarely does it have a call-to-action that tells people what to do. With a very simple tap-to-call button, you can solve these problems and literally double or triple the number of calls coming in.

Like many of the other techniques and tips you will find in this book, most are just simple tweaks. Once you can see the power of a large phone number and a call to action, you will wonder why more people don't think of it. The simple tweaks you make today will make you successful tomorrow.

The Power of a Tap-to-Call Button

I rarely see a service business website with a tap-to-call button. If you implement what I'm about share with you, then you will have a steep advantage over your competition.

This is probably one of the most powerful ways to make your mobile website work for you. It's very simple. When a visitor hits your website on a smartphone, you want the first thing they see to be a big phone number button that spans the width of the screen. This needs to be at the top of every page and needs to be accompanied by a call-to-action that says "Tap To Call!"

Does this idea of a call to action sound familiar? It's the same idea we discussed in Chapter 1. Just like with the desktop version, you want to make it brain-dead easy for them to contact you. It's even more important on smart phones because the visitor has an even shorter attention span. They are probably on the go and will just want a quick estimate. They have a problem they want solved and we want to be ready to offer them the solution.

We want prospective clients on the phone so we can book jobs and make money. Don't make them jump through hoops or work to get you on the phone. A confused mind will turn to the easy solution. Bottom line, you want to make it easy for them to do business with you.

Now that we have the essential usability elements covered, we can talk about some of the subtler customizations that can really make your site pop. In the next chapter, we will discuss the look and feel of your website and how it can help boost conversions even higher. Are you feeling the excitement of easily turning your website into a *Job-getting, Deal-closing, 24/7 Money-Making Machine?*

Chapter 3 Action Steps:

Test your website to make sure it passes the Google Mobile Test.

Decide on whether to use a separate mobile website or a mobile responsive website.

Make sure you have a Tap-to-Call button at the top of every page of your mobile or responsive website.

NOTES:

Chapter 4:

Look and Feel

You may wonder why I didn't start with this chapter. Shouldn't we first focus on the way the website looks before we start talking about conversions? The answer is "NO." As a web designer, you would think that pictures, layout, colors, etc. would be my primary focus, right?

When I first started my design career, that is what I thought too. With college level design classes, 95% of the focus is on how the website looks and how it makes the visitor feel. Once I started digging in and testing conversions, I realized that, in this industry, conversion elements will trump design every time. So, while design is important, it does take a back seat to conversion.

You are gaining the benefits of my successes and failures since 2009. You don't need to reinvent the wheel, just follow along and profit from my knowledge and experience.

That said, let's get into the look and feel of your site. What makes a website "Pop"? What gives a website that professional, modern feel that makes people say "Wow! I love this website"? What is that secret ingredient that says to a potential customer, "You can trust this company"?

Branding

If you want to build a long-term business that people remember, then you need consider your brand. An effective brand gives you an edge on the competition. But what exactly does "branding" mean?

> The Business Dictionary states: "Unique design, sign, symbol, words, or a combination of these, employed in creating an image that identifies a product and differentiates it from its competitors. Over time, this image becomes associated with a level of credibility, quality, and satisfaction in the consumer's mind (see positioning). Thus brands help harried consumers in a crowded and complex marketplace, by standing for certain benefits and value. Legal name for a brand is trademark and, when it identifies or represents a firm, it is called a brand name and corporate identity."

Simply put, your brand is the image you want to portray to the world. It is the promise you make to the customer. Who are you and what do you represent to the public?

Are you a high-end provider? Or are you the affordable provider? You can't be both and you can't be all things to all people. Both models work, but it will depend on how you want to brand yourself.

The foundation of your brand is your logo, your company colors and the layout of your website, as well as the content on your website. Let's break these down and address them individually.

Your Company Logo

Will a good logo make or break a business? No, but if you want something people remember then you need one that differentiates you from the competition. With branding, you want to be top-of-mind when someone thinks about your service.

We all have brand loyalties, whether it is a favorite restaurant, vehicle or smart phone. If we see their logo on a sign, advertisement, van or left side of a company shirt, that is instant brand recognition. When it's time to make a purchase, we tend to go to those brands that seem familiar and have built a sense of trust and recognition in our minds.

You want to have that same effect in your community. When people think of your industry or service, you want your logo to pop into their head. In a networking situation when someone asks for recommendations, you want as many advocates as possible out there referring you and your business. My advice is to spend a little extra time and money on getting a great logo that sets you apart.

We recommend that you find someone who specializes in logo design. Designing a website or a brochure is a completely different skill set than designing a logo. I consider myself pretty damn good at graphic design and web design, but when it comes to logo design, I turn to a dedicated professional.

Good logo designers have something special that can't be taught. Logo design is truly an art form. Each logo designer will have their own style and will be able to put the message you want to convey in a symbol and design.

It is not always easy to find someone that captures your feelings about what you and your business represent. I recommend finding one that understands your business and what you are all about. Find one that understands your brand and your promise.

I believe a good logo will determine the overall look and feel of a website. When considering a logo, you have to consider colors. The color scheme of your logo will set the stage for color scheme of your entire website. Some colors attract and some repel. Let's talk about how to choose colors that match your brand.

Your Company Colors

Color plays a major role in defining your brand. This visually obvious yet subtle aspect of a website has an important impact on the way your brand is perceived by the public.

Out of all our visual senses, color is the most influential, followed by shapes, symbols, and finally words. That is why I don't put much emphasis on sales copy for this industry. You are providing a visual image for your service, so let's focus on that.

Let's look at what colors mean on a basic level. People associate how they feel about your brand according to their personal experience with your services. By selecting the right color combination, you are taking a step in the right direction to effectively promoting your brand.

Basic Color Meanings

Blue: Trustworthy, Stability, Loyalty, Wisdom, Confidence, Trust, Friendliness, Preservation, Courage, Science.

Green: Calming, Freshness, Natural, Clean, Eco-Friendly, Completion, Protection.

Red and Orange: Urgency, Emergency, Power, Vigor, Passion, Activity.

(406) 493-1881

Black and Brown: Powerful, Mysterious, Elegance, Sophistication, High-end.

Yellow: Stress, Childish, Warning, Arrogance, Danger.

Pink and Purple: Romantic, Feminine, Soft, Sweet.

Based on these simple color signals, you can determine what feeling you want to convey with your brand and your logo. How do you want prospective clients to be drawn to your business? What is the unconscious feeling or emotion you hope the public will remember about your business when they see the logo, signage and website?

Now let's see how the logo and color scheme fit into the website by first starting with two different types of layouts.

Layout Options

After figuring out the color scheme of a website, we need to determine which style layout to use. Both the fixed width and fluid layouts are very functional. There may be many options out there to choose from, but this will give you insight to make a simple decision.

Fixed Width Layout

The fixed width layout is the classic website design style where a specific width is predetermined and then it typically is positioned in the center of the screen. On widescreen monitors, you will see a border or background where the website sits. On screens that are more square in shape, the background will not be visible and it will fill the screen. In this example you can see how the website sits in the middle with a faded background.

Fluid Layout

The fluid layout differs because there is no set width. It fills the screen from left to right regardless of the screen size. It will stretch and resize as the screen size changes. Many people prefer this option because it has more of a modern feel. These days most of the websites our company creates are in the fluid layout.

Pictures and Images

As we discussed previously, in this industry a very visual website will convert better than a text-heavy informational website. We will get more into pictures and video in the Trust section, but let's hit a few key points here to get your creative juices flowing.

If possible, use personalized photos as opposed to stock photography. When you get a few good pictures, they can be used over and over for all different types of marketing. I use the picture of myself in a nice polo shirt with a smile and a relaxed pose. I want people to know I'm a normal guy that is approachable.

Stock photography will work fine, but be absolutely sure you have permission to use them. Your site can be shut down if you are using photos without permission or giving attribution to the photographer or you can face fines.

You may be tempted to just right click on photos you find on Facebook or the web and copy them. I know you are now eager to get your website up and live, but it is better to get some quality custom photos taken by a professional photographer. These personal photos will really set you apart. You can find a local photographer on Cragislist.com for a reasonable price.

Try to match some of the colors in the photos with the colors in your logo and website color scheme. This will give the website a sense of flow and really help with the "Wow" factor.

Now that we have covered the major usability elements, it's time to get into a few of the technical aspects of your website. In the next chapter, we will move on to domains, hosting and website management. You are on your way to your very own website that will be a *Job-getting, Deal-closing, 24/7 Money- Making Machine.*

Chapter 4 Action Steps:

Consider hiring a professional logo designer that understands what your brand is about.

Decide if you want your website to have a fixed width layout or a fluid layout.

Consider hiring a photographer to take some personalized pictures that you can use on your website to further support your brand and connect with potential clients.

NOTES:

Chapter 5:

Domains, Hosting and Websites

Hosting, SEO, Google Analytics, Backlinks, Domains… When Internet guys start throwing around technical terms, it can sound like a different language. Sometimes they use that as a sales tactic or try to impress you with their knowledge.

They just forget that the average business owner doesn't deal with this stuff day in and day out.

Don't be intimidated. Regardless of their motives, there are a few terms you do need to be familiar with. You will need to have a basic understanding in order to make smart decisions and avoid wasting money. Even more important, you want to avoid having your website held hostage by an unscrupulous web designer or marketing company.

Understanding Domains

A domain is a unique address that people can type into a web browser to view your website. It typically ends in .com, .net, or .org. It's also called a website address or a URL. It's important to understand that this is not your actual website. It is simply an address that a website can sit on.

You can think of a domain like a street address and the website as the house that the address is assigned to. You never permanently own a domain. You pay to register your domain each year through a company like GoDaddy.com (highly recommended). Once it is registered to you, it will remain assigned to you unless you let it expire or sell the registration to someone else.

A lot of people get domains confused with website hosting. Registering a domain and registering hosting, however, are two different things.

Understanding Hosting

If you have a website, you will need pay a hosting company to provide space on a special web server. This allows people to access the website on the Internet. Hosting is just a space you are renting on a server so your website can be viewed live on the Internet.

You can think of your hosting like the lot that your house sits on. It is not the address and it is not the actual house. The hosting is simply the space that your website sits on. The fee you pay for the lot can be compared to Home Owners Association dues or yearly taxes on the land.

Understanding Websites

Ok, you think know what a website is. We all look at websites every day. But how does it play into this conversation? If we all know what a website is, then we need to be sure we recognize what it is not. It's not the domain address, and it's not the hosting space.

It's all the words, pictures, videos, links, etc. It's all the stuff people can see and interact with. As mentioned before, you can think of your website like a house. It's the physical stuff you can see, hear and interact with.

How should you choose a domain?

Before we get into the specifics of choosing a domain, there are a couple of issues you need to know about.

If your website is like your house, then the domain is like your address. You can't always get the domain you want. Someone else may have already registered it. Think of it like someone may be leasing the property. So before you can use your favorite domain, you need to check to see it it's "on the market" and available for you to use.

You can do a quick check online by simply typing in the exact domain name you wish to use in the address bar on your screen. If a website pops up on your computer, you're out of luck; that domain is taken and not available to you. I recommend using Godaddy.com to check domain availability.

If you already have a domain then don't worry about changing it. Having a domain with a solid history of one year or more is more important for SEO than everything I am about to discuss.

I see people spending way too much time worrying about getting the "perfect" domain. First, try to get the domain that is your exact business name followed by a .com (for example, www.BillsHomeService.com). This will be good for branding and in the past few years Google has been giving branded domain names a little boost in rankings. Like I said, though, it's not a deal breaker. If you already have an established domain, don't worry about it.

If your business name domain is not available, then you can always tack on a city or state name to make it unique to you. For example: if www.BillsHomeServices.com is not available, then go with something like www.BillsHomesServicesTexas.com. Once again, don't agonize over it. In the "Big Picture" it is not that crucial.

What About Exact Match Domains?

An Exact Match Domain (EMD) is a domain that is made of words that match popular search terms. It used to be a slick way to trick Google and get higher rankings for domains that matched popular search terms. For example: "Chicago Carpet Cleaner" is a very profitable search term to rank for in Google. In the past, if you had the domain www.ChicagoCarpetCleaner.com, you would have a sizable advantage in ranking very high very fast.

Google caught on to this game pretty fast and it just isn't a good option any longer. In some cases, it can get you into trouble as it is very easy to "over-optimize" an Exact Match Domain and acquire a nasty Google penalty.

I know I just used a couple of technical terms. This will make more sense when you read the chapters on SEO.

Things to consider when you are choosing a domain are to keep it as short as possible, make sure it is easy to spell, and avoid hyphens or dashes. Also, try to get .com or .net. Avoid all the new fancy extensions like .biz, .me, .co. There is less of a trust factor with both Google and consumers when it comes to anything other than a .com or .net.

How to Register A Domain

There are thousands of options when is comes to registering your domain. Do yourself a favor and use Godaddy.com. They are the leader when it comes to domains. They have amazing customer support 24/7 and are based in America.

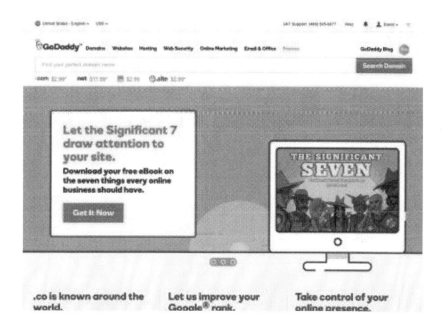

If it is your first time dealing with this stuff, just go to their website and call the phone number. They will step you through the process and get you up and running in about 10 minutes.

Beware, they have a very aggressive upsell program. Once you make your purchase, they will try to sell you all kinds of extra stuff that sounds important. My advice is to stick with the very basic domain service, which is around fourteen dollars per year. Just register the domain for two or more years and be done with it.

Keeping Control Of Your Domain

It is very important that you register the domain in your name. Don't let a web designer or anyone else register it for you. Would you put the title of your car in your mechanic's name? No, of course not. The same goes for domains.

I don't know how many times I have seen unethical web designers convince a business owner to let them take care of the domain registration. Then when it's time to get a new website, they are held hostage by that web designer because the registration is in the web designer's name. They own it and won't let it go or want to charge a ridiculous price to transfer it over. Or they go out of business and have disappeared from the face of the earth.

This can be detrimental to a business if you have an established domain that appears on Google search results, on website directories, business cards, van wraps, etc. If you have to start over with a new domain it can really set you back.

Choosing A Host

Just like with domain registering there are lots of options when it comes to hosting. It is very important to understand that, just like all service companies are not the same, not all hosting companies are the same.

If price is a major concern, then choose Godaddy. Since you probably already have your domain with Godaddy, it makes sense to keep everything in one place. The only drawback to using Godaddy hosting is that they are a budget hosting company, which means that although they will provide support for your hosting account, they will not maintain your website and provide fully managed services.

They do have a program called Managed Wordpress Hosting, but based on my research, it is not true managed hosting. They offer installation of Wordpress and some extra security features, but you still have to make your own updates.

I have also found that with Godaddy or other budget hosting companies, you will occasionally have slow load speeds when their servers are having problems or lots of traffic. This can hurt your business if it takes someone 10 or 20 seconds to pull your website up. Remember, people have short attention spans and if they don't get what they want quickly, they are moving on to your competitor's website.

If you want true managed hosting that is completely hands off with all updates taken care of for you, then spend the extra money and go with www.wpengine.com This is truly a hands-off option. They will handle everything for you, including all Wordpress updates. And they have blazing fast speeds and top-notch customer support.

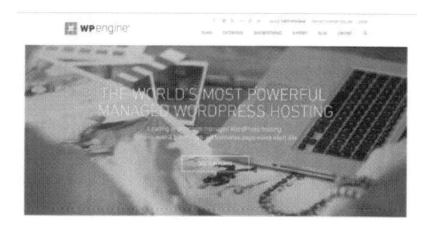

Some web design companies offer in-house hosting services along with their design services in order to make technical issues easier to handle and have more control over the entire process. Our company, Big West Marketing, offers a fully managed hosting service for these very reasons.

If you feel like you are working with a stable company, then this may be a viable option. Just make sure they offer true managed hosting so everything is taken care of for you.

Choosing A Website Platform

Once you have your domain and hosting set up, it's time to put the actual website up on the Internet. There are several popular website platforms to choose from including: Wordpress, Joomla and HTML.

Then there are the do-it-yourself options like wix.com or squarespace.com. Although many of these DIY options have come a long way in their software programs, you will still have many limitations. You will be limited when it comes to design, especially in implementing some of the crucial elements like big phone numbers with calls-to-action and a mobile tap-to-call button as discussed in earlier chapters.

I've already mentioned Wordpress as a website platform. In my opinion it is by far the best choice. Wordpress is the most widely supported web development platform in the world. Over 40% of all small business websites on the Internet are built on Wordpress. Our company designs exclusively in Wordpress because it gives us the greatest amount of flexibility when it comes to web design and search engine optimization.

Most web hosting companies will take care of the installation and initial setup for Wordpress at no extra charge. I highly recommend you have your hosting company do this for you in order to save time. But if you want to jump in and do it yourself, just visit www.wordpress.org to download the free startup files.

Note: Be aware that www.wordpress.com is an independent platform and is very different from what we are talking about.

The drawback to Wordpress is that there is a learning curve for those that want to build their own site. You are reading this book because you want to be successful in your own business. You want to do those tasks that show your skill and talent to the highest degree. You do so many things really well and that is where the bulk of your profit is going to come from.

It is very possible to create an amazing site yourself using Wordpress with little web design knowledge. Because you want to focus on what you do very well, however, you must ask yourself: "How much time do I want to take away from my business to do this?"

In most cases, it makes better sense to find a professional to take care of it for you, so you can be up and running as soon as possible. Remember the goal of the website is to be a *Job- getting, Deal-closing,*

24/7 Money-Making Machine. The sooner you are up and running, the sooner you are in a profit-making position.

Now that the technical stuff is handled, it's time to really set yourself apart from the competition by building trust.

Chapter 5 Action Steps:

If you don't have a domain, head over to Godaddy.com and register a domain according to the criteria in this chapter.

Decide if you want budget hosting or fully managed hosting.

- Godaddy.com and WPengine.com are highly recommended.

Decide on the web design platform you want to use to build the website.

- Wordpress.org is highly recommended.

NOTES:

Chapter 6:

Building Trust

This may be the most important chapter in the entire book. In my opinion, trust is the most vital factor when it comes to conversions from your website. On the surface, it seems that customers are most concerned with price, process, service guarantee, etc. Underneath all the rational thought, is the basic human desire to work with someone they can trust. Your potential customers are waiting for you to convince them that you are *THE* one company that can solve their problems.

We are going to talk about trust in the context of your website, but these principles can be applied to all aspects of your marketing. If you take the following information to heart, you will be way ahead of your competition both online and offline. We all like to do business with people we can know, like and trust.

Using Your Website To Establish Trust

It is very likely that when visitors land on your website, they bounce off within a matter of seconds. Why? These are the main four reasons that people are not staying on your website long enough to make a buying decision:

1.   Your website may have poor design and bad user experience (which we discussed in Chapter 2).

2.   Your website may be an online "brochure." It's static, flat and boring.

3.   Your website may be too busy and confusing. There are too many pictures, too many buttons, too much text, too many menu items and it's crammed together. There is no focus.

4.   Most importantly, your website may fail to convey trust. It may not make you or your business seem approachable and human. It's not engaging with the visitor. It doesn't make the visitor feel welcome.

So how do we change this and stand out from the competition? You want to give them a good feeling by personally greeting them. And at the same time you want to establish trust by showing them a clear path to answers. You want to prove that other people (like them) are satisfied and happy with you and your company. And you want to do all this within a few seconds so they stay on your website and pick up the phone.

Even though I tell my clients over and over to do this, most just won't do what I'm about to share with you. It is such an easy tweak, and yet many fail to put it into practice. If you are one of the brave ones, you will separate yourself and have a HUGE advantage. And it's so simple: All you do is put a quality picture of you (smiling) on the Home page. The photo doesn't have to be just you. It can be you and the family, you and the crew, you and your dog. Then next to the picture in quotes you give a short heartfelt "message from the owner."

Like I said, you must personally greet them and show that you are there to serve them and help solve their problems.

It's interesting that whenever I have a one-on-one consultation with a potential client, I start out asking about their business. Most people will have an amazing genuine story that explains why they really shine. I really love hearing that. Owning any kind of business that supports you and your family is a huge accomplishment. But when you go to their website, it's just flat and generic. It might look nice and professional but there is nothing personal.

Quality clients want to connect with someone trustworthy who will be coming into their home or business. A smiling face and warm message will establish this connection. And if you want to go even farther, make a personalized welcome video. I will show you how to use the true power of video in the next chapter.

So why do most business owners not do this? I keep hearing that they are too ugly, too old, too fat, or something along those lines. Listen,

I'm 5'6", chubby, balding and hate looking at my picture, but what I've come to realize is that it's the smile that makes all the difference. People tell me this. They say things like: "I saw your picture…" or "I saw your video and you seem like a good guy that I can trust."

Another reason business owners don't want to do this is because they don't want people to know they are a small operation. They want to compete with the franchises or the Big Brands head-to-head. If this is your goal then you are also going to have to spend like them. That means TV, radio, mass mail-outs, etc.

Do you have that kind of budget?

If you are a one-man-show or even a two- or three-truck operation, be proud of that. Quality clients want to work with people like you and that will never change. More and more, potential customers look for the local small business. They want to support their neighbors. The kind of clients you want to attract don't want the underpaid employee that shows up just for a paycheck and is in a hurry to get done so they can go meet their buddies to play video games. If they do want to use a Big Brand then they are going to call the Big Brand, not someone who is trying to look like a Big Brand that they have never heard of.

This strategy is also the best way to beat out bait-and-switch competitors. If that's not enough, it will also help you charge more for your services and weed out the bottom-of-the-barrel clients that only care about the cheapest price in town. No quality service business should charge dirt-cheap prices for their services. You work too hard to play that game.

So hopefully you get the idea: make it personal and make a connection. Be proud of you and what you have to offer, and you will be building a business to last a lifetime. Your pride and confidence will be an instant trust (and phone call) magnet.

Website Reviews and Testimonials

We have already discussed the importance of have a dedicated Testimonials page on your website, but you also want one or more short testimonials on your Home page from someone that fits the profile of your target customer. Who is your ideal customer? Who typically writes the check? If you put their picture next to the testimonial, you can expect double the results. Do you want to expect triple or more results? Then also include video testimonials!

Third Party Reviews and Testimonials

Local service businesses often underestimate the effectiveness of customer reviews on websites like Google and Yelp. According to an extensive survey from BrightLocal.com here is why you should care:

- 92% of consumers read online reviews

- 68% say positive reviews make them trust a local business more
- 40% of consumers form an opinion by reading just one to three reviews

You should definitely have a system in place to get online reviews. At the very least there should be links from your website over to the review pages on specific online directories such as Yelp.com or your Facebook Business page.

(406) 493-1881

There are also numerous third party review programs that will help guide customers to your directory pages, increasing the chances of them posting their reviews. This seems like a great idea, but there are drawbacks to these programs. Most of them are typically recurring monthly services ranging from $30/mo to $400/month and you have to learn a new piece of software. If you are not a techy person, it may be confusing and have way more bells and whistles than you will ever use.

Our company addressed this issue by implementing a simple program built in to all new websites we develop. We call it the Easy 5 Star program. It simply allows you to enter a customer's email, click send and wait for the reviews to come in. At the time of this writing, we have had amazing results. I use it myself every time we complete a job. If you would like more information, check out http://easy5star.com or call our office at 406-493-1881.

Trust Icons

Trust icons are simple badges or graphics that you place on your website. Examples include: Industry Certification, Association Memberships, local Chamber of Commerce, etc.

Use anything that looks official, even if they have no idea what it is. This is a psychological trigger that gives you instant trust and authority. You're not just a guy with a truck and a cell phone; you are a pro and have proof right here on your website.

The Guarantee

It is imperative that you offer customer satisfaction. Just a simple 100% Satisfaction Guarantee that shows you stand by your work. I know some websites will have a whole page dedicated to their complicated guarantee policy. And that is fine, but I think that is overkill. Keep it simple, mean what you say and honor the guarantee if you are ever asked to do so by a customer. You will be surprised at how many people will write a favorable review about a company who has had to redo work. Do it with a smile and they will be your cheerleaders forever.

(406) 493-1881

In summary, to establish trust on your website, implement a personal greeting, testimonials, trust icons and a guarantee. These simple improvements to your website are truly powerful and yet very simple and easy to do.

In the next chapter I will give you a step-by-step blueprint to creating a simple video that can boost your trust factor even higher and establish you as the authority in your community.

Chapter 6 Action Steps:

Put a personalized picture or video of yourself with a big smile and welcoming message on your Home page.

Make sure you have client reviews on your Home page, Testimonials page and other third party sites such as Google or Yelp.

Make sure you have trust icons and guarantees on the Home page of your website.

(406) 493-1881

NOTES:

Chapter 7:

Video Power!

Do videos really work? This is a question I get a lot and the answer is a definite "Maybe". I know that's not a very satisfying answer. You are probably thinking: "Joe, everyone says I need video. I watch video all the time. I'd rather watch video than read a bunch of text on my computer screen or phone."

Ok, so the simple answer is "Yes." But the problem starts when you use a blanket statement like, "Videos work great for marketing." That's the same as saying, "Websites work great for marketing". As we have already learned in this book, in order for a website to really work, it needs to be set up and presented in a specific way. In fact, a lot of the elements I teach about web design also apply to video.

If you create (or have someone else create) a professional-looking video with lots of stock pictures and some catchy background music, do you think that is going to connect with a potential client? The answer is "No." That's the same thing as setting up a boring generic brochure-style website.

(406) 493-1881

Now, imagine this: A video begins playing with background music. The owner of the company and his crew are getting ready to start the day. They are dressed professionally and it's obvious they are ready to work. It then shows ten seconds of a smiling customer talking about how amazing the company is.

The owner makes a few comments about how important it is that the customer is satisfied and how quality is a priority. There are several shots of completed work and then the video ends with a simple call-to-action, a phone number and a logo.

The entire video lasts about a minute.

Do you see the difference? The first video was boring and generic. The second video says "Hey, nice to meet you. We are people that you can trust. Let us know when you are ready to solve your problems."

Believe me, I have built my business on video. And I can say first hand that a short personalized video is worth tens of thousands of dollars. The great thing is that it's a little work up front, but once it's complete, it's done FOREVER!

It works for you 24/7. It's a powerful component of *The Service Business Money Machine.*

Do you have to have a video to make your website produce results? No, but it sure helps. And if your competitors do not have a video as described above, then you win. You will get the call before they do.

How to Make a Video Step by Step

By doing a little prep work you can increase the chances of your video being successful. You don't have to be the director of a major motion picture, but you are the producer of a customer-magnet video.

1. Decide on a specific day to film the video, preferably when the weather is nice and lighting is good. Is it an indoor or an outdoor scene? This will depend on the specific service you are promoting on the video.
2. List all of the people that will appear in the video. Examples are employees, top clients or family members. Make sure they are aware of the date, time and location.
3. List all of the props that will appear in the video. Examples are tools, equipment, vans and backgrounds. Gather them in one place.
4. List all of the locations and settings. Examples are workshop, office, customer's home and job sites. If you want to build a lot of local business, it is good to utilize recognizable locations in your community.
5. Create a very rough outline of how the video will play out. This may be a "story board." Watch other industry-related videos on Youtube.com to get ideas.
6. If there are going to be specific speaking parts, then create a very rough script. It is easiest to create bullet points so you are sure everything important is covered in a short amount of time.
7. Make your life easy and find a local video pro on Craigslist.org under Creative Services. You may have to pay them a few hundred dollars to film and edit. Check their references and ask to see some of their work. This will save you hours of headaches trying to figure out cameras, lighting and complicated editing software. Many times, they will have insight and ideas for props, locations, scripts and other elements that you may be struggling with.

I recommend paying them half of the agreed-on price at the filming and the rest when the finished product is delivered. Be aware that if you are paying by the hour, one minute of video may take several hours to edit. I prefer to pay by the project.

8. Once the video is complete, you will need to upload it to Youtube.com. To log into your YouTube.com account, use the same Gmail or Google login you use to log in to your Google My Business account. Google owns YouTube.com so the login information is the same and the accounts will be connected.

9. Once you log in to YouTube.com, click on the Upload button at the top of the screen. Then you will be able to browse and find your video file or drag and drop the file into the Video Upload box.

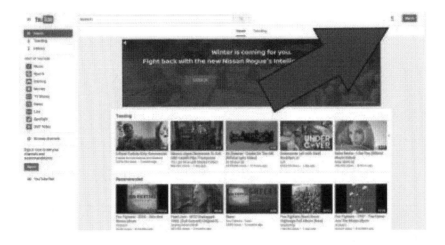

10. Next you need to optimize your video for Search Engine Optimization and to help with conversions if someone finds your video on YouTube.com.

    After the video upload is complete, you will be taken to a screen that allows you to make edits to the video. There are two sections that we want to work on here.

    - First, the Title. You want this Title to contain your primary service, the city you are located in and the name of your business exactly as it appears on your Google My Business listing.

    - Second, you want to move on to the Description box. Here you will add your website, your phone number and your physical address (optional if you work from home). You can also place the web addresses to your different Social Media accounts if you would like.

(406) 493-1881

Now that the video is published live on YouTube.com, you want to do what is called embedding it to your website. This can get a little technical. If you have a web designer, then you may want them to do this for you. If you want to do it yourself, then go to the page where your video is located on Youtube.com. Below the video, click Share, then click Embed. You will be given a box of HTML code that needs to be copied and pasted to your website.

If you are on the edit screen of Wordpress, then you will need to make sure you are in the "Text" tab, not the "Visual" tab. If you are using a platform other than Wordpress, you will need to check with their help department. Once this is complete, the video will now appear as if it is live on your website.

In closing, don't worry about making a cinematic Hollywood production. The power of video comes from how "real" it is. Feel free to make mistakes, and remember to smile. When speaking to the camera, just imagine you are having a conversation with a potential client.

If you have implemented everything up to this point, then you now have an amazing high-converting, lead-generating website, a virtual

Money Machine. In the next chapter let's discuss how to close the deal once a visitor picks up the phone to call you.

Chapter 7 Action Steps:

Create a simple 1 to 2 minute video script and outline. Then plan when and where you will do the filming and any people or props that will be involved.

Hire a reasonably priced videographer from Craigslist.org to do the video work and editing.

Upload your video to YouTube.com and make sure it is correctly formatted for Search Engine Optimization. Then embed the video on your website.

NOTES:

Chapter 8:

Closing the Deal

Although this chapter is not directly related to websites or marketing, it will offer you extra assistance in building your business. All of the tips and techniques in this chapter will prove helpful in accomplishing our overall goal, which is to get you jobs and make more money.

What if you increased your jobs by just 20% by establishing some simple phone scripts? That could easily add up to thousands of extra dollars over the course of the year, depending on your volume, upsells, pricing, etc.

Before we begin I want to explain where I'm coming from. A while back I dedicated an entire day to calling 30+ service companies in response to a marketing launch I had released. My goal was to give free consultations for a new service we were providing at the time.

I was shocked by the lack of phone skills. Only one out of four companies I called picked up their phone; instead the call was allowed to go to voicemail. In several cases the voicemail was not even set up, or had a voice mailbox that was full. And the ones that did pick up had very weak answers and not one had a solid script.

This is good news for you because chances are your competitors are weak on the phone as well. They are losing business daily and probably don't even know it.

Imagine this as a secret weapon you have been handed. If you can "Wow" potential clients on the website and continue the "Wow" factor when they call, then you are almost guaranteed the job.

Why Should You Listen to Me?

I've had several jobs in the past that involved customer service and phone sales. I was trained to connect with the customer and close a sale. I naively took for granted that phone skills were common sense and something most people just did automatically, I remember we were always having some kind of ongoing training. There was always something new to discover about phone sales and building relationships with customers.

Back then, I thought it was kind of a waste of my valuable time to learn about customer service. Now I realize the reason the companies spent so much time and money on service skills is because it is not common sense, it is a skill. Skills need to be learned and practiced daily in order for them to become automatic habits. When you become a better salesperson and learn to connect with others, it will enhance every aspect of your life, personally and professionally.

Those rare companies that invest in customer service skills make their money back many times over. Their salespeople have more sales and less rejection, and they become top producers, simply because they know what to say and how to say it.

So, I'm going to break down what I've learned and what I applied to my own business.

6 Essentials Tips to Closing Deals on the Phone

1. **Just Pick it Up** – If you want more work then pick up the phone. I know you don't want to pick up the phone during the middle of a job, but if you're a one-man show then you need to do it anyway. You need to pick up on weekends, in the evenings and anytime it rings, even when you don't feel like it.

Of course, if you have a receptionist, spouse, business partner or someone else that can pick up the phone, then that's ideal. I've seen the husband-wife arrangement and that works really well, but whoever is in charge of the phone needs to pick it up every time it rings.

The chances of closing a job decrease dramatically if they don't get you right away. Many people won't even leave a message. They will just call the next company and if they answer the phone and offer a solution to the customer's problem, the business is most likely theirs.

2. **Voicemail** - Set up a professional voicemail message. Don't mumble or just say the name of the business. State your name and then the business. If you absolutely can't pick up the phone, then you need to have a professional voicemail message setup. Make sure you smile on the message– more on that in a minute. Keep it short — 15 to 20 seconds.

VERY IMPORTANT: Call people back ASAP. Check your voicemail at least three times per day. People who call your phone are looking for a solution to their problem. If you wait too long they are gone!

3. **Answering Script** - This will make you sound more professional and confident, and get you on and off the phone faster. Have your FAQ (Frequently Asked Questions) ready to go. Having short consistent answers to questions will make all the difference in closing the sale and getting the business. Check out our website or give us a call for a sample phone script.

4. **Pricing Chart** - If you do price quotes over the phone, then have a pricing chart ready to go so you're not fumbling for prices, giving inconsistent quotes, etc. I noticed that when I started doing this, customers were much more responsive because they knew I was professional. I was giving them real pricing and not just quoting based on my mood or how well I liked their voice.

Also, if you are just pulling numbers out of your head on the fly, then it's hard to remember what prices you quoted. It just doesn't sound professional when you say, "Well, I think we could do it for...". Having a consistent pricing system will allow you to grow your business.

5. **Smile when you talk.** This is one of the most important and easiest things you can do. There have been countless studies by customer service experts who agree that when you smile, it comes through on the phone. Smiling and speaking in an approachable tone of voice ALWAYS results in increased sales and customer satisfaction. Some companies even put mirrors next to the employee phones as a reminder to smile while talking on the phone.

6.   Use their name a minimum of three times — This is another relationship builder that has all kinds of research behind it. Using someone's name at least three times during the call will instill trust and make them feel more comfortable doing business with you. After all, we like doing business with people we know, like and trust.

I prefer to use their name at the beginning. I always ask them to spell their name as early as possible so they will know I am taking notes and am concerned about solving their problem. You will want use it once during the conversation and then at the very end: "Ok, Susan. I will see you Tuesday at 1pm"

I know it's hard to form new habits if you have been doing things a certain way for a long time. This may sound like a lot of work, but it's really not. All skills, just like riding a bike or using a piece of equipment, take practice and consistent use in order for it to become automatic action.

Just implement these tips one at a time. Once they become habit you won't even think about them, and I promise it will make a HUGE difference.

So far, we have covered all of the elements to creating an amazing money-making website that instills trust and gets the phone ringing, and then how to close the deal once they call.

Are you getting excited about implementing these tools into your business toolbox? Have you grasped the idea that your website is truly a *Money Machine*?

The final section of the book will address traffic to your. This will include Google traffic using Search Engine Optimization, Facebook marketing.

Let's get started!

Chapter 8 Action Steps:

Create a simple phone answering script to be used by anyone who picks up the phone.

Make sure you have a professional-sounding voicemail set up for those rare times you don't pick up the phone.

• Check messages often and call back ASAP.

Learn and implement the 6 Essential Tips to Closing Deals on the Phone.

(406) 493-1881

NOTES:

Chapter 9:

SEO - Understanding the Game

Search Engine Optimization (SEO) is the closest thing to "automatic marketing" that you will find. When someone searches for your service on the Internet and your business ranks high on the first page, then you will get more business.

I have experienced the power of this first hand from running my own service business. Depending on the search engine terms used, I would be getting three to five calls per day from the website alone. Remember, this is in Missoula, Montana with a service area of only around 70,000 people.

In the big metropolitan areas, some companies are getting 10, 20 or even 30 calls per day from their website. That's not taking into account referrals, repeat business and other advertising and marketing. The correct use of SEO and a high-converting website is like a salesperson that works for you 24/7 rain or shine.

I'm not just bragging to impress you with what we have done. Our company, Big West Marketing, has helped hundreds of happy clients who have doubled, tripled and even quadrupled their business using these techniques. I am sharing our methods and systems because we want to help you to create your own *Money Machine*.

Why SEO Is Different for Service-Based Businesses

SEO is the same for all businesses, right? It's the same for Carpet Cleaners, Dog Groomers, Online Jewelry Stores and Walmart.com, right? The answer is absolutely not. For some reason this myth is perpetuated over and over by almost all marketing pros.

There are hundreds, if not thousands of techniques, strategies, tools and tricks to rank a website at the top of Google. All these so-called marketing experts want you to believe they have the magic solution and the missing piece to the ranking puzzle.

The truth is there is no single solution to effective SEO. There are many factors involved and one of the biggest considerations is the type of business. Ranking a brick-and-mortar retail shop requires a much different approach than ranking an online ecommerce store. Ranking a service-based business that goes out to client locations requires a vastly different strategy from a retail store or online store.

Why is this so important? Because most information you find on SEO is very generic and won't apply to your situation. You need specialized information specific to your type of business. Otherwise you will drive yourself crazy trying to understand and implement techniques and strategies. Most of those don't apply to you, and that can cost you hours of wasted time and thousands of dollars in wasted money.

If you had a brain injury, would you go to a foot doctor for advice? No, you want a neurosurgeon who understands and has experience with your specific injury. The same goes for SEO. My expertise is in SEO for service-based businesses like yours, and that is our focus in this book.

I'm not going to teach you how to be an SEO expert for all types of businesses. You are not going to find sweeping generalizations about SEO. I am going to give you a very specific blueprint for ranking a service business website.

Google is King!

When I use the term SEO I am referring to ranking as high as possible on the first page of search results on Google.com. This involves using search terms that generate traffic, clicks and phone calls.

Why only Google? As of this writing, over 90% of people use Google to find a local business. Google is king! Google is where you will get the most traffic and the most customers, so that is our focus throughout this section.

That said, SEO should not be your only marketing tactic but rather a part of your complete marketing strategy. You should still be working on reminder and referral programs, face-to-face networking, Facebook, postcard mail-outs etc. You never know when Google will make a change. You don't want to have all your eggs in one basket.

One of your BIG goals when it comes to marketing (besides getting the phone to ring) is to funnel every potential client to your website. If you have implemented everything in this book, you are on a path to success. You will have established enough trust and credibility to demand higher prices, separate yourself from the competition and close the deal.

Before we jump into the how-to lessons, let's clarify the different components of SEO and then establish some basic vocabulary.

The Crucial Difference Between Paid Ads, Local SEO and Organic SEO

When someone searches for a local business on Google.com, three different types of results will appear: Paid Ads, Local Results and Organic Results. Let's take a look at each so we can decide what is most important and then spend our time, energy and money as efficiently as possible.

1. **Paid Listings** – Also known as Pay-Per-Click (PPC) or Google Ad-words, they appear at the very top of any results page. They will be designated by the word "Ad". These listings are not part of SEO. These are simple advertisements that businesses pay for on a per-click basis.

   They only receive an average of 10% of the total clicks and hold little trust with the searcher. Although they can be somewhat effective for certain services in certain cities, they will not be a topic of discussion in this book.

2. **Local Listings** – These types of listings go by many names including: Maps Listings, Google My Business and Google Places. They all refer to the section of listings below the Paid Ads. They can be identified with a map image and each listing will have star ratings associated with each one. These results are where you will get the most traffic to your website.

An average of 80% of searchers will click on these listings first. They hold the most trust and therefore when I talk about SEO or ranking on Google I am primarily referring to these listings. Remember, our goal is to get the maximum amount of traffic and phone calls. These listings are where the money is made.

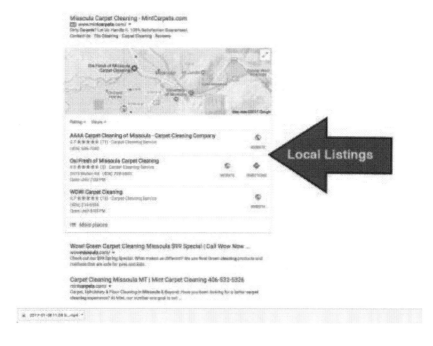

3. **Organic Listings** – These types of listings appear below the Paid Ads and Local listings. Usually a searcher will have to scroll quite a way down the page to even see the organic listings, especially

(406) 493-1881

on a mobile device. Although they do hold more trust than the Paid Ads, their low placement results in an average of only 10% of the clicks for local business searches. Therefore, we will not focus too much on Organic listings, but they are part of SEO so I will address some ranking factors.

How Much Work Is Involved?

The bulk of the work is done up front and after that, minor maintenance will be required to maintain rankings. This is almost like residual income. Work hard once and reap the rewards for a long time.

There is a common myth circulating throughout the SEO industry that to rank a website, you have to be constantly adding fresh new content or blog posts to your website every day, week or month. Although this may be true for some types of websites, it does not apply to small local businesses. Trust me, I have thoroughly tested this idea and can attest that fresh content doesn't help a small business rank higher, especially in the Local listings.

What is the Guarantee that you will Rank on Google?

Google is a third-party platform. When dealing with any third-party platform, it is impossible to guarantee anything 100%. There are so many factors that come into play, including the history of your business, the history of your domain, your physical location, etc.

There are no guarantees with any kind of marketing, whether it be postcard marketing, word of mouth, print advertising or even TV and radio. So unfortunately, no one can guarantee anything in marketing, but you will be setting yourself up for the best chance of success if you follow my system.

The information I'm about to share with you will give you the best possible chance of ranking any type of service-based business on Google. The more you know, the better job you will do with your website.

Google Penalties

Before attempting to rank your website, you should be aware that your website may be tagged with Google penalties. How will you know if you have been penalized? This is something that is often overlooked by business owners and SEO companies, but is crucial to your success. This little-known fact is especially true for service based businesses and contractors.

In my experience the majority of service companies work out of their home and have changed addresses, phone numbers or business names at least once during the life of their business.

(406) 493-1881

These small changes create inconsistencies across the Internet that can negatively affect your website rankings on Google. One of the most important ranking factors is clean, consistent information across the Internet. That is how Google decides if you are a stable, reputable business. If you have conflicting information, it can create penalties and drop your rankings.

Another way to get penalized is poor SEO link building practices. Link building will be explained in detail in chapter 11. If you have worked with one or more SEO companies in the past, they may or may not have created links from other websites and/or profile listings that Google considers spammy. A common practice is to create multiple phony business listings in attempt to rank in areas that you don't have a physical location. These days this will get you into trouble.

In the next two chapters, we will address how to clean up and remove penalties that may be holding you back.

SEO is a game, but it is a game that you can win once you understand the rules and how the playing field is laid out. Like in any game, the team has players with differing skills and talents. Those teams that have a knowledgeable coach to guide and direct them have an advantage. I hope you will consider me your coach and trust my experience and my hard-won skills to help you win.

In the next few chapters I will teach you all my top strategies and tactics for getting your business and website to the top of Google.

Chapter 9 Action Steps:

Understand that SEO for service businesses is very different from other types of businesses

Make sure your address is listed to autheticate that you are a local listing.

• Local listings account for 80% of clicks.

Make sure you update your information and maintain consistancy across the internet to avoid Google penalties.

(406) 493-1881

NOTES:

Chapter 10:

On-site SEO

In order to make SEO easier to execute, let's work together to make sure you understand some basic definitions. What I provide here is only the essential SEO jargon. If you want to drive yourself crazy, you can find thousands more confusing and unnecessary terms relating to SEO.

This book wants to cut out the fat and give you what you need so you rank your website and turn it into a money machine.
I acknowledge that at first this may still seem overwhelming. Breathe deep; it will all start to make sense soon. The goal of this information is to get you started on a do-it-yourself program or as a resource when looking to hire someone to do it for you.

On-site vs. Off-site SEO

The SEO process can be divided into two separate activities.

1. On-site SEO refers to things you do to your website directly. This involves the text, pictures, schema and keyword metadata. Don't panic. I will explain these terms below.
2. Off-site SEO involves activities that are not directly related to your website. This will include things such as setting up a

Google My Business page, a Facebook business page, online directory listings and link building activities. These terms will be covered in the next chapter.

In this chapter, we cover the On-site factors starting with Keywords.

Keywords

The first thing you need to understand is the concept of Keywords (aka Search Terms). A Keyword or Search Term simply refers to a word or phrase that someone types into Google to find you. Even though the term Keyword makes you think of just one word, it is more often a series of words. They are usually phrases that are typed in when someone is looking for a resource or an answer to a problem.

These Keywords need to be placed on your website so Google knows what to rank you for. Examples: "Plumber Missoula" or "Roofing Contractor Indianapolis IN"

IMPORTANT TIP: Make sure you put the service before the city name in your Keywords. More people than not, search type the service first and city second so in doing it this way you increase your chances of ranking for a more popular Keyword. Example: "Fencing Company Denver" instead of "Denver Fencing Company."

Meta Titles

You need to make sure these Keywords are placed in your Meta Title – sometimes referred to as Title Tags. You can see this on any website by hovering your mouse over the tab in your browser.

In Wordpress you will typically place this within the Page Edit screen. It is important that you include Keywords in the Title Tags of all your different service pages, not just the Home page.

Some Wordpress themes will allow you to do this, but if not, you will need to install a free Wordpress plugin called Yoast SEO. To learn how to install a plugin go to YouTube.com and search "How to install Wordpress plugin." There are many easy-to-follow videos to step you through this process.

If you are using other platforms, then you will need to search around to find the Meta Title section. Just insert one Keyword or phrase per page followed by the Business Name. Example: **Plumber Missoula – Bobs Plumbing and Heating Services.**

Resist the temptation to insert multiple Keywords into the Title Tag. Google is very sensitive to this and may issue a penalty for "Keywords Stuffing." If you want to rank for more Keywords, then I suggest simply creating additional pages to target those Keywords. To rank in multiple cities, please see Chapter 12 for an in-depth explanation of what Google will and will not allow.

Unique Content

The next important onsite SEO element is unique content – meaning the text or words on your site. It is a good idea to have at least 250 words or more of unique content on each page you want to rank. Is your content unique? Don't be so sure. You MUST run every page of your site through a free service called Copyscape.com. If it shows more than 125 words on any one page being duplicates from another website, then it could be hurting your rankings.

We have found that a lot of business owners will copy and paste content from someone else's website then make a few changes and call it their own. If it doesn't pass Copyscape.com, then you may be hurting yourself. Keep in mind this really only applies to pages that you want to rank.

At the time of this writing it is not important to worry about pages such as the About Us, Contact Us, FAQ, etc. Primarily it is the service pages that you will want to rank. If you don't want to do the writing yourself, you can hire inexpensive "ghost-writers" on services such as Craiglist.org, Textbroker.com or Fiverr.com.

However, you may need to test a few writers until you find one that speaks in your "voice" and is knowledgeable about your industry.

How Franchises Get Away with Duplicate Content

Whenever I start talking about duplicate content penalties, I frequently get questions on how some bigger companies can continue to use duplicate content and avoid Google penalties.

Google does not treat all business or all websites the same. Websites and businesses that have been around for years and have proven themselves to Google as solid established entities will receive some leeway. They get special treatment when it comes to duplicate content and other penalty-related issues.

Google's goal is to weed out spammy websites or fake businesses that are new to the scene. If you are a small locally based operation, it is best not to test Google on this. Just trust my experience. We are positioning your website to have the best chance of ranking.

How to Fix Duplicate Content Issues

What do you do if you see duplicate content on your site? For our clients, we immediately hire a writer to rewrite the content or come up with something new. We then run it through Copyscape.com and if it passes, we replace the content on that specific page.

What if you see that someone else has completely copied your stuff? First, contact them with a cease and desist order. If they don't comply, then contact their hosting company. If they still don't comply, the host will possibly suspend the website until the issue is resolved.

The Mobile Factor

So, we have already spoken about your site being mobile friendly for usability reasons, but it is also crucial for SEO. Since Google's big mobile update, I've seen sites drop 10 spots or more simply because they are not mobile ready.

And, just like with unique content, don't assume your site is mobile friendly. Find out for sure by doing a Google search for "Google Mobile Test." Do a quick check with Google's Free Mobile testing tool. See chapter 3 for more information.

Social Media Links

The last thing I want to mention on this topic is placing links from your website reaching out to your social media business pages. When I say links, I mean when you click on a graphic on your website, it takes you to a new website or page on the Internet.

For example: you will want to have a graphic for Facebook somewhere on the website so that it appears on every page. When a visitor clicks on that graphic, they are sent to your Facebook Business Page (which we talk about setting up in the next chapter).

Don't get carried away here. We all know there are 100s of social media sites out there, but the most important are Google My Business, Facebook, Yelp and possibly Angie's List.

Just put links from your website to the ones you have set up. For tutorials on how to do this in Wordpress, go to YouTube.com and search for "How to create a link in Wordpress." Keep in mind we are not talking about posting anything to your social media sites; we are simply linking over. For SEO purposes, you just want to show Google that you have properties on the Internet other than your website.

Image Alt Tags

Image Alt Tags, also known as Alternative Text, are associated with the pictures on your website. Google cannot read images and so you have to tell them what the photo is about. It also aids people with visual disabilities to identify pictures. Keep in mind that Alt Tags are different than the caption.

(406) 493-1881

With Wordpress, click on the edit icon for an individual picture and you will see an Alt Tag field that allows you to insert your Keyword. You can easily insert Keyword(s) into the Alt Tags similar to the page Title Tags, but make sure to use only one Keyword (or Keyword phrase such as "HVAC Contractor") per picture per page to avoid "Keyword Stuffing" that can result in a Google penalty. The method for editing Alt Tags differs from platform to platform.

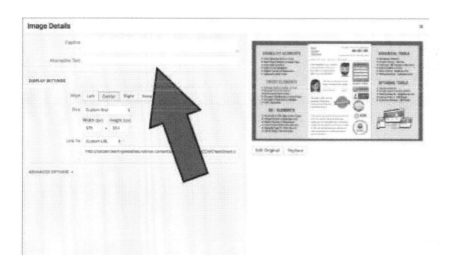

URL Permalinks

The words contained in your website's URL or web address changes from page to page. These are called Permalinks and are an often-overlooked ranking factor that should not be ignored. Make sure the words after the slash have variations of your Keywords for that specific page. An example would be:

www.yourwebsite.com/carpet-cleaner-services

You can set the Permalinks in the Wordpress Dashboard under Settings.

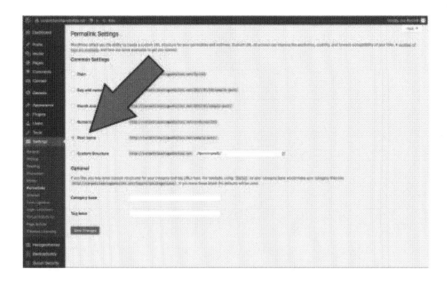

Other platforms will vary in how Permalinks are set. You will need to research your specific platforms settings in this regard.

Schema Code

In the next chapter, we talk about the importance of having a correct Business Name, Address and Phone number on all of your listings across the Internet. It is also important to have it correctly set up on the website itself. This is done using something called Schema code.

To generate this code, simply do a Google search for "local business schema generator." There are many free websites that will help you generate the necessary code. At the time of this writing our company, Big West Marketing is using www.microdatagenerator.com

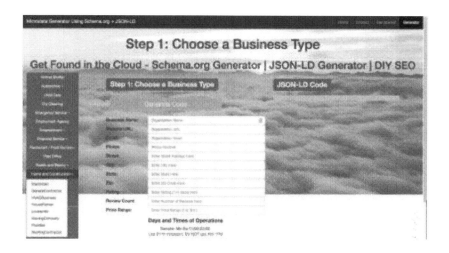

Once the code is generated, I recommend copying and pasting it into the footer of your website so it shows up on every page. This step will make it easier for Google to match your correct Internet profile information with your website information.

Content Keywords

There is a lot of debate when it comes to putting Keywords into the content of each page of your website. At the time of this writing Google's penalty filters are very sensitive, so my opinion is that less is more.

I recommend writing content that is targeted to the visitor, not for Google. Instead of repeating the Keyword over and over throughout the text, use variations that sound natural.

What Not to Worry About

If you search the Internet, you will find hundreds of free SEO analyzer programs. They ask you to enter your website and then give you a report with lots of errors and corrections that need to be made. In my opinion, most of this information is useless. It is either outdated or is a marketing ploy to get you to spend money to "fix" these errors.

A lot of the metrics these reports talk about sound very important and may have been valid at one time. Some of the more common metrics they will talk about include the following list:
- Meta Description
- Meta Keywords
- Keyword Density
- H Tags
- Subtitles
- Image Titles
- Image Descriptions

At the time of this writing, I have found that the factors listed above are not critical to Google ranking success, especially when it comes to ranking in the Google local listings section.

It is easy to get bogged down with all the thousands of possibilities and opinions when it comes to SEO. My advice is to keep it simple and focus on the big important factors that I discuss in this book. Don't worry about getting everything perfect, just aim for pretty darn good and you will still be way ahead of your competition.

Now that we have covered all the most important On-site SEO factors, it's time to go beyond your website. We are going to start working with Off-site SEO that will really get your website visible to Google and help boost your business to the top of the rankings.

You may be feeling overwhelmed with TMI or "Too Much Information." Relax! This will fall into place. Remember, most of your competitors will have thrown in the towel by now. 90% of success is just showing up and not giving up. You are on your way!

Chapter 10 Action Steps:

Identify Keywords you would like your website to rank for and place them in the appropriate locations on your website.

Use Copyscape.com to verify that your website has unique content to avoid Google's duplicate content penalties.

Make sure you have correctly set up Social Media links, Permalinks and Schema Code on your website.

NOTES:

Chapter 11:

Off-site SEO

In this chapter, we are going to go over step-by-step exactly how to rank a service business website on the top of Google. Most people see SEO as something reserved for computer experts with high-level technical skills. Of course, the SEO pros that charge money for their services want you to believe this. The truth is that SEO is actually very simple as long as you know the basics.

90% of the information you hear or read about on the Internet is complete BS that has been regurgitated over and over. Most people have not actually tested for themselves what works and what doesn't.

Remember, the way I tackle both website conversions and SEO ranking is by testing for myself. The information I am about to share with you is the result of my extensive testing since 2009. Don't let the simplicity fool you. Just because something is simple doesn't mean it is easy. It is real work that takes time and patience. It can be tedious, but the payoff is well worth it. Like I said in a previous chapter, SEO is the closest thing you will ever find to automatic marketing.

The purpose of this chapter is to give you the building blocks to implement your own SEO campaign. On the other hand, if you are

(406) 493-1881

looking to hire an SEO company, you will know how to weed out the pros from the scam artists.

It's A Changing Game

Be aware that SEO changes as Google introduces ranking updates, so some of the information here may be outdated, depending on when you are reading it. That said, the general principles I present should remain true for years to come. As new information becomes available, I may release updated versions of this book or videos on my blog. Be sure to sign up for my email list to stay current on the latest SEO information. Call our office for more information at 406-493-1881.

The first step to any Off-site SEO campaign is to set up your business account with Google.

Setting Up the Google My Business Account

To begin, go to this website: **business.google.com**
You will be prompted to get started. If you do not have a Google account, you will create one from scratch and will be assigned a Gmail account as the username. If you already have a Gmail account you can use that to start. On this page, you should also see a support phone number to call if you have any questions or want someone to walk you through the process.

Once the business account is set up and you begin to enter your business information, there are a few things to keep in mind:

1. Make sure you fill out everything as completely as possible. This includes hours of operation, photos, forms of payment, etc. Don't leave anything blank.

2. If you are working from a home address, make sure you select "Yes" for: "I deliver goods and services to my customers at their locations." This will hide your address from the public. Google requires this for residential addresses. If you select "No" then it could affect rankings.

3. Make sure the Business Name, Address and Phone Number are EXACTLY how you want it to appear across the Internet. Google will compare your information to every listing you have on the Internet. If this information is inconsistent then it will affect rankings. This is the biggest issue I see with service-based businesses not ranking, so get it right the first time. More on this later in Chapter 12.

4. After you complete the setup, Google will mail a postcard to the address you entered. It is very important that you keep a lookout for this card. It will have a special verification code that you must enter into the account before it goes live on the

(406) 493-1881

Internet. If you fail to do this, your Google My Business account will not be activated and ranking in the Maps section will most likely not happen.

Setting Up Your Facebook Business Page

After the Google My Business account is complete, a Facebook Business Page needs to be set up. In order to create the Business page, you must first have a Personal Facebook account under your name. The Business Page will be set up under your personal account. Don't worry, the public will not be able to see that your personal name is associated with the Business Page unless you specify in the Settings.

To create the Business Page, log in to your Personal Facebook Account and in the upper right-hand corner, click on the little down arrow and then select Create Page. The process is very straightforward and only takes a few minutes. It is important that you enter the EXACT same Business Name, Address and Phone Number to match your Google My Business account. If you already have a Facebook Business page, check to see if the information matches your Google My Business account EXACTLY. Change it if necessary.

Citations and Other Online Directories

If you research SEO for local businesses, you will often come across the term "citation." A citation is simply a mention of your Business Name, Address and Phone number somewhere on the Internet. The more citations you have on quality Internet directory websites, the better chance you have of ranking in the Google Local listings section. At this point you have set up the two most important citations with Google and Facebook.

Now it's time to blast more citations out to the Internet. Luckily there are some nifty tools that will help speed up this process. The two that I like are Yext.com and Moz.com/local. These are both paid services (check websites for current pricing) that allow you to register your information one time and they will submit to many of the top online directories for your business. This can be a huge time saver. Once again, it is important that all of your information matches EXACTLY with your Google My Business account in order to have the best chance of ranking.

(406) 493-1881

How To Clean Up Citations

I mentioned that having inconsistent information is a major issue service-based businesses have when trying to rank on Google. When we partner with a client and start an SEO campaign, the first thing we do is a thorough citation audit.

This means we scour the Internet to find anything and everything we can about the client's business. It is very common to find loads of misinformation, duplicate listings, incomplete citations, old addresses, old phone numbers and different variations of business names. If you have been in business for any length of time, this may describe your situation. Here are the most common reasons this happens:

- Your business moved physical locations
- You used tracking phone numbers at one point
- You hired an SEO company to create citations or get listed on online directories
- You changed your local phone number
- You used an 800 number and not a local number
- You have different trade name or business name variations
- Your listing was incorrectly submitted and picked up by other sites
- Someone with your company set up the listings without knowledge of citation consistency (this is very common)

I highly recommend you start your own citation audit to determine if this is holding you back. Be aware this requires a significant amount of time and tedious work, but it is necessary if you want to rank your business in the Google Local listings section. Here is the step-by-step:

1. Make a list of all possible variations of Business Names, Addresses and Phone numbers your business might have used since the beginning of time.

2. Start doing separate Google searches for everything you came up with in step 1 and record everything you find in an Excel spreadsheet. I like to have the following columns: Directory Listing, Business Name, Address, City, State, Zip, Phone, Status, Notes

3. Use Moz.com/local to get a listing score and see if they find anything you missed. If so, mark it on the spreadsheet.

4. Use Brightlocal.com to complete a Local SEO Checkup to find anything you missed. If so, mark it on the spreadsheet.

5. Use the Whitespark.ca Citation Finder tool to find anything you missed. If so, mark it on the spreadsheet.

Once the audit is complete and you know where you stand, it's time to begin the cleanup process.

This can be a little frustrating because all of the directories have their own systems and methods for accessing data and making changes. Some will allow you to claim accounts and set up new login information, some will require email requests and others may require phone verifications.

As you move through the cleanup process for each incorrect citation, I recommend you use the same email that you registered with Google. Be sure to take detailed notes in the Note column of your audit spreadsheet.

Be aware that when you submit your information through tools like Yext.com or Moz.com/local, they will take care of some cleanup. Most of the time, however, you will have to complete the work manually or hire an experienced SEO company to do the work for you. Also note that after a citation has been corrected, it could take weeks or months for Google to review that listing and update your rankings.

When you are sure that your business citations are submitted and as consistent as possible across the Internet, it's time to power up your website with backlinks.

What Are Backlinks?

Backlinks are the turbo boosters that push websites to the top of the Google search results page, both in the Local listings and the Organic listings. They are very powerful, but they must be created slowly over time and in a very specific way.

They must also be the last part of your SEO campaign. If you have sloppy onsite SEO or lots of inconsistent citations, then backlinks will be virtually useless and can possibly have a negative effect on your rankings.

Imagine a race car with bald tires, no brakes and faulty steering. What would happen if you installed a brand new powerful engine into that car? What chance would you have of winning the race? You would be lucky if you even made it to the finish line without crashing and burning. The same principle applies to your website rankings. Make sure everything is clean and in good working order. Take care of the basics before applying power.

To understand what a backlink is, just go to almost any website on the Internet. Do you see words that are colored blue or purple? What about pictures that you can click on? When you click on them they link over to other websites or other pages? If so, those are backlinks.

Some people just call them links. Don't be confused; they are the exact same thing. So, a backlink is anything on a website that is clickable and links you over to another website or webpage.

Google scours the Internet every second, every minute and every hour of every day. Their job is to index the millions of backlinks on the Internet to determine which businesses have the highest quality and most relevant backlinks pointing to their website. Each one of these backlinks is like a vote. Google tallies up the votes and starts to rank websites based on this information.

Pretty simple, right? Yes, the concept is simple but to acquire good quality relevant backlinks can be a challenge. And remember I said quality relevant backlinks. This is extremely important. If you do a Google search for "buy SEO backlinks" you will be inundated with companies trying to sell unknowing business owners low quality backlinks that will most likely give you penalties instead of rankings.

My advice is to steer clear of anyone trying to sell backlinks. Take the time to do it right or find a reputable SEO firm to do it for you.

How to Build Backlinks

There are many ways to build backlinks but there are only a few safe ways that I have identified since I started working with SEO in 2009. Once again, things change in SEO all the time, but at the time of this writing, what I suggest here are the best and most powerful ways to build backlinks for a local business.

The key to building powerful backlinks is value exchange. You are basically going to be asking local and industry website owners to give you a valuable backlink. In exchange for that backlink, you will be giving them something of value. This process isn't difficult, but it is real work.

Let's look at the two types of backlinks we are going for.

Local Backlinks

Since you have a local business, it is important to acquire locally based backlinks from websites from within your community. Examples of these are local associations like the Chamber of Commerce, business groups, news websites, community blogs and non-profit organizations. These types of organizations are frequently looking for new articles or content to publish on their websites. If you can provide a valuable article or something of interest then they will most likely agree to give a backlink to your website.

Another option is to offer a trade for your services. Do they need your services in exchange for a backlink?

A third option is to simply ask them if you can buy a backlink. Make them an offer. Would they take $50 or $100 to simply put a backlink from their website to yours? Many times the answer is "Yes."

Industry Backlinks

In addition to local backlinks, Google also likes backlinks coming from relevant industry-based websites. Examples of these are news websites, trade publications, industry blogs, equipment companies and supply companies.

Once again, many of these website owners are looking for content to publish on their websites. Can you provide them a valuable article in exchange for a backlink? Can you hire a writer to create the article for you?

One of my favorite link building techniques I used for my business is the testimonial exchange. I contacted every equipment and supply company I had ever done business with. I asked the person who had the power to make the decision to give me a backlink in exchange for a review or testimonial that they could publish on their website.

We know that quality testimonials are gold to any business. This applies to people you buy from as well.

All you have to do is ask.

Another very powerful technique involves creating your own network of quality industry relevant websites that link back to your website. This can be a lot of work and will cost a significant amount of time and money. And once it is up and running, it will require frequent maintenance. It's not realistic for the average business owner. I want to mention it because it works and is one of the techniques we use to rank websites for our clients.

It basically involves finding old abandoned domains that already carry authority with Google. We use a tool called RegisterCompass.com to find the domains and then evaluate the domains using the tools Majestic.com and OpenSiteExplorer.org.

Once we find a domain we like, we use online auctions such as Godaddy Auctions or NameJet.com to bid on and purchase the domains. When we own those domains, we build industry- related websites and blogs with unique quality articles and videos. Within these are articles, we link back to our client's websites. This gives us complete control over the quality and number of backlinks coming in.

In conclusion, backlinks are powerful engines that boost website rankings. They are essential for any business that has significant online competition. It will take some work prospecting and reaching out to community and industry- related website owners, but the rewards are high rankings, phone calls and a steady stream of work.

I know SEO is unpredictable and not for everyone. It is my goal for you to explore the best options when it comes to cashing in on Internet marketing. In chapter 13, we will get into Facebook marketing, which can also be a very effective way to increase traffic to your website

Chapter 11 Action Steps:

Set up your Google My Business account and get it verified with a postcard.

Set up your Facebook Business page.

Create and clean up citations to match your Google My Business information.

Implement a link building outreach program to local and industry website owners.

(406) 493-1881

NOTES:

Chapter 12:

Google My Business FAQ

At our company, Big West Marketing, we get a lot of questions on what Google will or will not allow when it comes to ranking in multiple cities. The following information is based on a combination of many hours of testing and talking with Google employees. I have used that information and hands-on experience to rank hundreds of local service-based businesses in the US and Canada since 2009.

This information does NOT apply to Organic Ranking or Google AdWords Pay-Per-Click.

What <u>CAN</u> I Use as an Address To Rank in the Google Local Listings?

- Single Residential House Address
- Single Residential Apartment Address
- Commercial Office Suites or Units
- Single or Multiple Commercial Address(es)

What <u>CAN'T</u> I Use as an Address To Rank in the Google Local Listings?

- Combination of Residential and Commercial Addresses
- Multiple Residential Addresses (Exceptions for Large Franchises)
- PO Boxes, UPS Mailboxes or other Mailbox companies
- Virtual Offices
- Commercial Address Inhabited by Another Business

Where Can I Rank?

You must have a physical address that is able to receive mail, in the city you want to rank. You must list the actual city, NOT an adjoining suburb, nearby city or county. It MUST be the city that the post office uses when delivering mail. Google will send you a physical postcard to verify that it's a legitimate address.

What About Surrounding Cities?

Sometimes Google will rank your business in neighboring cities if there is little competition; however, this will most likely be in the Organic Listings. If you want to rank in large, competitive cities or suburbs, then forget about ranking in the Google Maps section unless you have a physical address in that city or suburb.

Can I Dominate the Entire Metro Area in a Big City?

In order to rank a single business in multiple cities, you MUST have a legitimate, verifiable commercial address for each location. These locations can't have other businesses currently occupying them. To rank multiple residential locations, you must be part of a large franchise.

Or

The only way to really "Fool Google" with multiple residential locations is to have completely unique Google Accounts, Business Names, Phone Numbers, Addresses, Websites and Listings Across the Internet. They must appear to be completely different businesses to a human or Google. For most small businesses, the time and cost involved is just not realistic.

How Is My Competitor Getting Away With It?

From time to time Google will miss the mark and someone breaking the rules will get away with it, especially if they have been ranking for many years. However, it is becoming less and less common because Google now has teams of human employees scouring the Internet for fake business listings or obvious violations of their guidelines.

I have seen people get away with "Fooling Google" for years at a time. I have also seen people get their entire accounts shut down or marked as spam. So, if you are going to take a chance and try to "Fool Google", just be aware there is a certain level of risk involved. Typically, if you get away with breaking the rules, it will only be for a short time. In my opinion it is not a good long-term solution.

What Happens When I Move or Change My Phone Number?

The MOST important factor in local SEO is having consistent information across the Internet. Therefore, changing your business name, address or phone number is the BIGGEST action that a business makes that affects Google Local Listings section ranking. That's why it is very important to keep track of ALL your usernames and passwords for EVERY directory or website.

Real SEO companies will put most of their time and effort into creating and maintaining this consistency. The reason most SEO companies don't do it (or do it incorrectly) is because it is hard, grueling, frustrating, time-consuming work. Regardless of whom you work with on SEO, be sure consistency is addressed and tracked throughout the process.

If you have any more questions, please contact our office at 406-493-1881. We are here to assist you in turning your website into a *Job-getting, Deal-closing, 24/7 Money-Making Machine*".

Chapter 12 Action Steps:

You must have a physical address that is able to receive mail in order to rank in that city with Google.

- Both residential addresses and commercial addresses are valid BUT not in combination

To rank in multiple locations you must have multiple verifiable addresses in EACH of the areas you wish to rank.

- These must be commercial addresses UNLESS you are part of a large franchise.

Make sure your information is consistent across the internet. This is the most important factor in local SEO.

NOTES:

Chapter 13:

Facebook Marketing

In the world of Internet marketing, Google is King. But in the past couple of years, Facebook has also become a viable lead source for many types of service businesses. Marketing on Facebook is very different from Google.

With Google, potential clients are searching for your service. In contrast, with Facebook you are pushing your services to them.

That said, the customer you get from Google is going to be more likely to spend money because they are looking for a solution to their problem, while the typical Facebook lead is either not interested or not ready to buy yet. They need to get to know, like and trust you.

So how do we make Facebook work? In my opinion, the key to Facebook success is timing. The chance of a potential customer viewing your ad at the exact moment they are ready to buy is slim to none. You will need to be showing up in their newsfeed on a continual basis. So, when the time to buy does come, your business is at the top of their mind.

There are two primary methods for a business to market on Facebook. Both methods can be very profitable when executed correctly. The method you choose will depend on your personality and how you choose to spend your time. The first method is free, but will cost you time. You will need to be working on Facebook almost every day. The second way involves paid advertising. It will involve some up-front time to get set up and a little time each week to change up the ads and settings, but far less time that the free method.

Which Method Is Right for You?

Let me ask you this: Are you already on Facebook every day? Do you enjoy using Facebook to communicate with friends and family? If the answer to these two questions is "Yes", then you may have some success with the free method. If you don't enjoy Facebook and you want to use it strictly for business purposes, then I highly recommend the paid advertising method or hire a marketing firm to do it for you.

The Free Method

(406) 493-1881

To market your business on Facebook without spending money, you will need to make a name for yourself. I recommend using a personal profile to do most of the posting instead of a dedicated business page. You still want to have a business page, but posting from the business page will only reach 10% to 20% of the people who "Liked" or "Followed" it. A Facebook "Like" or "Follow" is created when someone finds your Facebook Business. If people like what they see on your page, they can give you a "thumbs-up" by clicking a button that says "Like." This automatically enrolls them to "Follow" your page, meaning your posts will be inserted into their feed at no cost to you.

The reason for this is that Facebook wants you to pay to reach your audience. Furthermore, it's much more difficult to get people to Like your page as opposed getting them to accept a friend request. I recommend setting up a separate Facebook account for business. I have two accounts under my name so I don't annoy my friends and family with my business posts. It works great.

The way to really make this method work is to inject your personality into each and every post. This means lots of personal pictures from your smart phone. Use lots of faces of people, animals and local landmarks. You don't want to come off as a marketer; instead you want to be friendly and tell stories.

My good friend, Sid Graef, owns a very successful multi-truck service business here in Missoula, Montana. He is one of the best Facebook marketers I know, and his rule of thumb is to make all posts valuable, helpful or relevant. Once in a while you can throw in a special offer or some sort of pitch.

I recommend you post every day during the week. Only one of those posts should be directly promoting your service.

You can also run contests for discounts or freebies, but make sure people have to engage. It can be in the form of trivia or identifying a local landmark. You want people to participate and have fun. That's really what Facebook is about. If you can work with that mindset, you will get more business.

The Paid Method

If you are like many business owners, you don't have the time or the desire to hang out on Facebook every day. If this is the case, then buying advertising on Facebook may be the way to go. When done correctly, it can generate some steady business.

Remember, I mentioned that timing and repeated exposure is the key to Facebook marketing. The way to accomplish this is with a feature called Retargeting. When someone clicks one of your ads, they receive a piece of code called a pixel on their browser.

This allows you to repeatedly send ads to the same people over and over. Most likely they were interested in your service, but were not in buying mode. But if they see your ad six more times in the next month, you have greatly increased the chances of them picking up the phone and calling you.

Retargeting is so important when it comes to Facebook Ads that I recommend not spending any money with Facebook unless you have this set up correctly.

There is definitely a learning curve when it comes to setting up Facebook and Retargeting Ads. Facebook has some very helpful tutorials. You can also find hundreds of helpful how-to videos that give step-by-step instructions on YouTube.com.

(406) 493-1881

Facebook updates the Ads Manager interface so often that it probably will have changed several times by the time you finish reading this book. The important things I want you to take away from this chapter are the general strategies so you can jump in with a game plan instead of going at it blind.

Secret Bonus Strategy

Here is a strategy that I have come up with to easily double or triple the effectiveness of each and every Facebook Ad. Instead of running ads from your business page like most businesses do, you want to create a separate page that is all about local business reviews in your city.

Then you want pick your ten favorite businesses and write a review post for each one of them. This can be a restaurant, a mechanic, a friend's business, etc. It doesn't matter which ones you choose; you just want the new page to have some solid content so when someone checks it out, they will see that it is a legitimate review page.

From now on when you run ads, choose the review page instead your business page. The ad should be a recommendation instead of a pitch. It should say something like "We recommend Elite Home Remodeling for their amazing service…blah blah blah."

The reason this strategy works so well is because it appears to be coming from a third-party source. Everything should be written in the third person. It is called third party credibility. The trust factor is much higher than if it comes from the business itself.

That's it! Play with it, use it, modify it and get those calls coming in. At this point you should have enough ammunition to really make your website take off. In the final chapter I want to bring it all together so you can take action and get your *Money Machine* to really start working for you.

Chapter 13 Action Steps:

Decide if you want to go with the free Facebook marketing method or the paid advertising method.

If you go with the free method, open a separate Facebook account and start building your audience and credibility.

If you go with the paid advertising method, implement the secret bonus strategy to capitalize on third party credibility.

(406) 493-1881

NOTES:

Chapter 14:

Bringing It All Together

There are three big takeaways from this book. 80% of the people who buy this or receive it as a bonus will never get this far in the book. Of the 20% of you smart and ambitious entrepreneurs who read it, 80% will be inspired and really want to follow the blueprint. However, statistics and experience tell us that only 20% of that 80% will actually put into practice the principles I have shared with you. The rest will get distracted or fall back into old patterns and habits or just give up.

Do you realize that if you utilize these three takeaways today and commit to following the steps I have laid out for you, you will succeed? You will stand head and shoulders above your competitors.

1. The first takeaway is that you need to make sure your website is very user-friendly. There should be no question in the visitor's mind of what it is you provide and how to reach you. I hope that my explanations and examples provide a blueprint for how you can effectively create a website yourself or be in a good position to hire it out to a qualified web designer that understands you and your brand.

2. The second takeaway is that in order to really set your website apart from the crowd, you need to establish some genuine trust with your potential clients. I hope this book has inspired you to go personal with your website and your business. I hope you understand the competitive advantage that can be unleashed for your business when these ideas are taken to heart and implemented correctly.

3. That leads us to the final takeaway. In order to really make the website do its job, you need to get people to visit the site. You need real qualified traffic. It is my hope that using the tactics in this book for both Google and Facebook, you will have the foundation to do it yourself or be educated enough to hire the right marketing company for the job.

Over the years, business owners have struggled with the switch from the Yellow Pages to the Internet. The new age is upon us and it is time to embrace this change. It's time to ride the wave and capitalize on this new and exciting form of marketing. Those that understand the journey toward progress will surely become the new industry leaders.

It is my hope that you will be one of those leaders.

Joe Burnich

READY FOR YOUR FREE 30 MINUTE CONSULTATION?

($97 Value)

Now that you have finished *The Service Business Money Machine* you may have some questions.

GIVE US A CALL NOW AT

406-493-1881

or visit

www.BigWestMarketing.com

Made in the USA
Columbia, SC
09 August 2019